Uncover Your Recovery

Uncover Your Healing

Maura Bertotti
and Ann Merli

UNCOVER YOUR RECOVERY by Ann Merli and Maura Bertotti

Published by IG Introspections, an imprint of Inspired Girl Publishing Group, a subsidiary of Inspired Girl Enterprises.

www.inspiredgirlbooks.com

Inspired Girl Publishing Group is honored to bring forth books with heart and stories that matter. We are proud to offer this book to our readers; the story, the experiences, and the words are the authors alone.

The authors have tried to recreate events, locales, and conversations from their memories. To maintain their anonymity in some instances they have changed the names of individuals and places, they may have changed some identifying characteristics and details such as physical properties, occupations, and places of residence to protect the privacy of the people involved.

The conversations in the book all come from the authors' recollections. They are not written to represent word-for-word transcripts, rather, the authors have told them in a way that evokes the feelings and meanings of what was said so that the essence of the dialogue is accurate.

The authors and publisher do not assume and hereby disclaim any liability in connection with the use of the information contained in this book.

This book is written as a source of information only. The information contained in this book should by no means be considered a substitute for the advice of a qualified medical professional, who should always be consulted before beginning any new diet, exercise, or other health program and before taking any dietary supplements or other medications.

Products, books, trademarks, and trademark names are used throughout this book to describe and inform the reader about various proprietary products that are owned by third parties. No endorsement of the information contained in this book is given by the owners of such products and trademarks, and no endorsement is implied by the inclusion of products, books, or trademarks in this book.

The Twelve Steps and the Twelve Traditions are reprinted with permission of Alcoholics Anonymous World Services, Inc. ("A.A.W.S."). Permission to reprint the Twelve Steps and the Twelve Traditions does not mean that A.A.W.S. has reviewed or approved the contents of this publication, or that A.A. necessarily agrees with the views expressed herein. A.A. is a program of recovery from alcoholism only - use of the Twelve Steps and Twelve Traditions in connection with programs and activities which are patterned after A.A., but which address other problems, or in any other non-A.A. context, does not imply otherwise..

ISBN: 979-8-9897899-3-1
Editorial Director: Jenn Tuma-Young
Copyeditor: Janelle Leonard
Cover Image: Michael Parker

Creative Directors: Ann Merli and Maura Bertotti
Substantive Editor: Natalie Papailiou
Cover Design Concept: Ann Merli and Maura Bertotti
Book Production: Jasmine Hromjak

Printed in the USA

Library of Congress Control Number
2024933555

Dedication from Ann

This book is dedicated to all the people who walk through life wounded in their hearts, find the bravery and courage to look within, take action, make changes, and transform their lives.

Dedication from Maura

My recovery started from deep pain.
My pain started from tremendous loss.
I dedicate this book to
My Heart,
My Angel,
My Dear, Dear Mother,
Patricia McNamara Bertotti

If it feels like déjà vu, it is!

We repeat concepts throughout
this book on purpose.
Repetition is our secret sauce for
lasting change and transformation.

Contents

Begin   A Message from Maura & Ann   ix

Highlights   What We Will Be Exploring, Addressing, and Diving Into   xiii

Guidance   How to Use the Tools in this Book   xv

Chapter 1   What Is Uncover Your Recovery   1

Chapter 2   Uncover Your Curiosity and Awareness   17

Chapter 3   Uncover Your Truth   33

Chapter 4   Uncover Your Emotions   51

Chapter 5   Uncover Your Behaviors   73

Chapter 6   Uncover and Discover Your Higher Power   89

Chapter 7   Pulling Together Body, Mind, and Spirit   105

Chapter 8   Healing Tools to Consider   121

Chapter 9   Resources, Favorite Quotes, and Poems that Helped Us Along the Way   137

Chapter 10   Healing Journey Stories from Ann and Maura   153

Acknowledgements   163

About the Authors   171

SPIRIT

by Ann Merli & Maura Bertotti

Spirit is the Universal Breath of Life.

It's the Universal Life force that co-creates with us.

It has no beginning and no end.

It emanates through time and space.

Spirit is what calls us to itself to remind us,

Love is the highest Light there is.

Spirit is the Supernatural Divine Force of All that is.

It is where we all come from.

It is what we are all surrounded by.

It is within, and without.

It is every essence of who we really are.

If only we'd realize this truth.

Our breath and life pulse this reminder:

We. Are. Spirit.

A Message from Maura & Ann
Before You Begin

The words we have written, the methods we have described, and any and all material in this book came to and from us personally. In most instances, information was given to us in meditation, or through direct channeling from Spirit, or through our individual, personal experiences. Because we believe in the collective consciousness of the universe, some ideas may seem familiar to you. We believe the healing path, when entered into with integrity, will hold the same thoughts and ideas that are collectively available to all of us through divine source. Due to this belief, we are now using our unique voices to express how we perceive the healing path and the tools, methods, and ideas that were gifted to us uniquely. We honor the universe and all the other healers on the planet. The gift of healing is innately ours, given to every single one of us, directly from divine source.

Please be aware that delving into this book may be challenging. Support is important. We suggest that you surround yourself whenever possible with supportive friends, family, self-care, and things that will help keep you safe as you go through this process and journey. We will also be providing many supportive resources along the way.

The world is not a one-size-fits-all type of place for healing. No one religion does it, no one program, organization, or person does it. If we look with open eyes, and all of our other senses, nature tells us this same thing. Nature has an abundance of opportunities in all its glorious wonder. Plants, animals, rocks, sky, earth, water, sun, moon, all of it contributes to healing as a whole. When we stay on a path of healing, marvelous things can happen. We also need to expand outward to see what else can help us. We are each unique beings with unique needs. When the world tries to control our healing in a limited approach there can be lack, rigidity, and blocks. We believe this is not what Spirit has intended for our healing journey.

Expansive thinking and curiosity brings us to the awareness that different paths will resonate for each one of us. This may go against the grain of established recovery programs and can change the way we look at healing from the whole body, mind, and spirit system. *Uncover Your Recovery, Uncover Your Healing* is exactly that.

In our process, and throughout this book, we invite people to get to know themselves, inside and out. It's an opportunity to uncover the blocks and overall conditioning that led us to disharmony in the first place. When we are given permission to take off the cloak of labels that have followed us through life, we can see an endless array of possibilities before us. We don't just have to work within the confines of using such things as therapy, prayer, yoga, family/societal constructs or expectations. We can free ourselves to explore in new ways.

This book is for everyone. It is designed to reach through multiple layers and across many categories. It has limitless potential. Since we are all experiencing many different situations stemming from hurts, traumas, mental and physical ailments, labels, grief, stigmas, disappointments, heartaches, losses, challenges, relationships, finances, family, etc., this work opens up an opportunity which is inclusive and accessible for everyone, without limitation.

We wrote this book as an invitation to walk you through a powerful and life-changing process. There is no time like the present to plant new seeds for healthy and positive change. As you move through this work, the newly planted seeds will grow, change, and expand little by little over time. This is the formula for vital growth and healing. In the past we, the authors, have made unproductive choices ourselves, which we have learned so much from. We want to share that knowledge with you. We don't have all the answers. Each question asked in the chapters requires action from you, the reader— active participation. Active participation for us means we no longer hand over our healing to someone else to fix. We now actually participate in our own healing process.

We ask ourselves the questions, we do the work, and this level of work invites us directly into the uncomfortable. This discomfort is where we can work together to uncover the wounding, and to share the investigative tools that have worked and continue to work for us. Bringing ourselves and you into balance and harmony, just like the seeds we are planting that bloom and blossom over time. This is an opportunity to take an honest look at your challenges and finally understand what they mean. We intend this book to be used as a source, a guide, and a toolbox, filled with information and real-life stories that can support you on your sacred journey of healing.

We want to extend a formal invitation for you to join us on the path to uncover your *own* recovery. When Spirit asked us to do this work, we accepted the invitation ourselves. We have been recovering individually, as well as working through this process together. We have learned along the way that we need to incorporate compassion, kindness, respect, and self-care. Giving ourselves an opportunity to approach this important work with gentleness, patience, mercy, and grace. It is paramount. We are building a bridge from here to healing. We now invite you along on this amazing journey with us.

We talk a lot about Spirit throughout this book. We created Uncover Your Recovery because there were both parallels and differences within our individual experiences. We realized every person has their own unique combination, their own personal prescription to heal. And by bringing our methods together, we started opening up to the infinite possibilities for individual healing. Recovery becomes a lot clearer when we learn that it's okay to take different teachings from different modalities. There is a saying, "take what you need, leave the rest." The truth is you first have to give yourself permission to choose what resonates for you from certain programs, modalities, and teachings. You may think these pieces don't fit together when in actuality you are creating your own beautiful mosaic.

We both grew up in the Roman Catholic Church. Our traumas and grief led us to dive even deeper into our faith and spirituality. Between the two of us, we have logged thousands of hours training, both ourselves and others. We've worked with clients locally and around the globe, teaching classes, workshops, leading circles, performing ceremonies, holding sacred rituals, and so much more. We have a combined background in Reiki/energy healing, massage therapy, yoga, mediumship, intuitive and psychic development, weight, and nutrition support, and so much more. We love the Blessed Mother, Jesus, Buddha, Quan Yin, the Angels and Archangels, the moon, the sun, the trees, the earth, the ocean, the animals, all the Light that is. We bring in teachings from all kinds of spiritual realms, messengers, guides, and teachers. We are now extending the invitation from Spirit to you, to find your path, to uncover the treasures buried deep within you so you can find your peace and Uncover Your Recovery.

Here are the key points we will be exploring, addressing, and diving into:

Uncover Your Curiosity and Awareness – Together these are some of the first tools to create change. Unhealthy patterns create unhealthy behaviors. Using new action tools can change your life. Both personal awareness and self-inquiry help us to identify our starting point.

Uncover Your Truth – Healing starts with truth. We come into this world with other people's beliefs and truths. Learning what is true for us and not for others is a crucial step in our process. We have the opportunity to be honest and clear with ourselves.

Uncover Your Emotions – Emotions are one of the main keys to recovery. When we deny or hide our emotions, we set ourselves up for unhealthy behavior patterns. It is necessary to find healthy ways to identify and express our emotions. This is an empowering practice to develop.

Uncover Your Behaviors – Unhealthy behaviors can be challenging patterns to break. Within our behaviors lie the information we need to change. We need to examine and identify our unhealthy behaviors for significant change to happen.

Uncover and Discover Your Higher Power – We believe in a spiritual power greater than ourselves. We also believe that everyone has a right to explore this for themselves. Start by thinking about what terms you are comfortable with. A Higher Power/Higher Self can change as you grow and heal and can be anything you believe in, as well as a source of comfort and support.

Uncover Working With Your Body, Mind, and Spirit – By working with these three significant aspects of ourselves, together we will integrate all the tools that make recovery possible.

Uncover and Build Your Own Recovery Program – Putting all the components together, you will discover your own individual unique healing plan that works for you.

Resources – We provide additional resources, information, and links for added continued support.

How to Use the Tools in this Book

At the end of each chapter, you will find three important opportunities that have served us well in our own individual journeys.

Permission Slip – Sometimes in life we might not realize that we need to give ourselves permission in order to break old patterns that keep us stuck. Fill out these slips like we did. Print your name and sign your permission slip.

Invitation/Challenge – Write, doodle or jot down something that you find significant in each chapter.

Self-Care Checklist – Find time to take care of yourself. These are things that we may not be familiar with doing for ourselves. We need to actively participate in our healing. You can change your self-care choices at the end of each chapter.

This checklist comes in two forms. One is in list-form the way Ann prefers it, and the other is in scattered-form the way Maura best relates.

Which style do you prefer?

These are empowerment exercises to make healthy and positive changes for your life, so please don't skip these steps. Use them as your active participation, creating a hands-on experience for deeper introspection and healing.

Ann's Story

Just when you thought it was safe to venture out into the world without therapy.

My road to health has been a weaving, turning, and twisting journey that continues daily. Without the help and support of therapy I honestly don't know where I would be. With that said, there was a time when I thought I was doing great and stopped going to therapy for about five or so years. I felt good, life seemed manageable, and then it wasn't. In the year 2006, my life turned upside down in lots of emotional ways. I ended a six-year relationship and entered into a long-distance relationship with my current husband. In November of 2006, I found myself signed up for a weeklong intensive "retreat" at a place called Onsite in Cumberland Furnace, Tennessee. This retreat was not what I expected. There was no spa, aromatherapy, candles, incense, or fancy bathrobes. There was my ignorance and naivete of what I had just signed up for. Along with forty of my closest friends that I didn't know, we were placed in four groups of ten. We would spend the next seven days with these ten people, unknown to us, some names not real, without awareness of occupation or story, in a room with a therapist and just ourselves.

As the days unfolded, we would work with our therapist who was trained in experiential therapy. This type of therapy uses tools, activities, and other methods to recreate present and past experiences to uncover them, and to heal them at a deeper mind, body, and spirit level. The work that went on in that room for seven days was the most profound experience of my life. It intensified emotions that I had thought I had dealt with in psychotherapy. We used role play, body movement and we physically felt our feelings. This was not something I had ever been exposed to. It is what brought me to be able to write this book, to uncover more deeply in my body where there was more healing that was needed, not just in my mind.

The one thing I had not planned on though was the level of intense emotions that would rise up when I arrived home. I had no therapist to come home to that would help me. Again, when I went, I was pretty igno-

rant of what I was getting myself into. The program was called Learning to Love Yourself, how hard could that be? Insert sarcasm and laughter. I was on the edge constantly, emotions like a roller coaster, angry, angry, sad, sad, happy, happy, then up and down again. It was so overwhelming. I wanted to quit my job, run away from home, and yell and scream. I could not get comfortable. In credit to the program, they did reference in the initial paperwork that it would be good if you were working with a therapist. I thought, "me, I'm good, I did so much therapy before." But oh, how wrong I was. I needed support, stat. Through my medical doctor, I found a new therapist. I owe him a debt of gratitude. Through his therapy we used more body centered therapy or as the current term is used, somatic therapy. Somatic therapy is a unique form of therapy that focuses on the mind-body connection to help bring about change. The changes I experienced in my body, mind, and spirit would allow me to do the biggest healing work of my life. I still see him on occasion, as needed. The tools he gave me to learn to self-regulate and manage my stress are tools I use every day.

Moral of the story. Get help. Be curious, interview your therapists, find someone that resonates with you. If you've been doing talk therapy for a long time, change it up with a more somatic therapy. Our mind is powerful, but our bodies hold so much. Working with this kind of therapy is not always easy, it invites us to be embodied. Most of us like to stay in our heads, distracted away from unpleasant sensations of feelings. I get it. Been there. Support, unconditional support, I firmly believe is one of the most healing things in the world. Allowing another to sit with our pain and not try to manage it for us, but to allow us to express it in a safe and supportive space, is one of the most sacred things to behold.

"*The woods are lovely, dark and deep.*
But I have promises to keep,
And miles to go before I sleep."

~ ROBERT FROST
Stopping by the Woods on a Snowy Evening

MAURA'S MESSAGE FROM SPIRIT

The Ocean told me a story today.

Crashing or calm, my power is strong.
Huge rising swells. Gentle waves, and salty smells.

Passionate life, bottom to top. Rhythm that will never stop.
Across the beaches, the tides, the sea . . .
A Universe of its own, within me.

Vast, powerful, moving, feeling . . .
Strong and deep, filled with healing.

You. You are the Ocean.

CHAPTER 1

What Is Uncover Your Recovery?

"The journey of a thousand miles,
begins with a single step."

- LAO TZU

Uncover Your Recovery is a system designed to identify and heal the challenges we each face in our lives. Multiple situations can hold us back from our shining success and freedom, and together we will walk you through a powerful, life-changing process. We will be looking at the actions, compulsions, behaviors, and addictions in our lives and where the challenges may be hidden. There are things you may not even be aware of within our unhealthy behavior patterns. This is inclusive and accessible for everyone without limitation. This is a way to recover from your own personal, challenging life experiences. The changes that come along with this work will be a freeing, authentic, and much welcomed alternative. It is time to heal like never before.

Uncovering Your Recovery is a journey that begins with you, taking a look at all the things you believe, think, feel, see, hear, and do in order to recover your true self that is already inside, waiting for you to start. That is what real recovery is all about.

Patience is underrated in our immediate gratification world. We need to have everything now. Think about how often you get annoyed waiting in line almost everywhere you go, waiting for a text, email, waiting for food, coffee, smoothie, or a drink. Impatience is thriving, the faster technology is the faster we want to go. We need our news now, immediately. We need to feel better now, immediately. You can put Band-Aids on your healing process by distracting and medicating yourself, but the concepts of patience, gentleness, and kindness seem remote and unattainable.

Patience is a practice. Like all practices, it takes time. You didn't learn to read or walk right off the bat, it took time. Nature is a great patience teacher. You plant a seed, it goes in the darkness of the earth, you water it, energy flows and it starts to grow. It uses more energy to burst through the soil, and the sun supports that growth. It takes time for seeds to grow. We are the same when it comes to healing. We might need some dark time, but with love, support, and nurturing, we can blossom to our fullest potential.

We invite you to practice patience, kindness, and gentleness toward yourself.

The very things you needed from others
you can gift toward yourself. You are worth it.

Recovery is a process, an act of change that can make a significant difference in your life. Recovery is not limited. It is a goal to improve, regain, return, and restore balance. It is also so much more. Most people associate the word recovery with substance use and addiction. Recovery touches almost every area of our lives, from mental health, physical illnesses, broken hearts, financial situations, childhood wounding, ancestral and generational traumas, and so forth. Recovery looks at our compulsions, behaviors, actions, etc. and gives us a great chance to evaluate the experiences that have shaped our lives.

What are your first thoughts when you hear the word recovery? What is the image that comes to mind? When you say the word recovery out loud, how does it make you feel? Do you feel uncomfortable? Do you notice any shift in your body, like anxiousness or tightness? Maybe you didn't notice anything at all.

We are encouraging you to shift your perception of the word recovery. We've had countless clients in our practices express that the concept, the word, the idea of recovery often has a negative connotation. Does it have the same effect if you say, "I just recovered from surgery, or I recovered from the cold I had," as it does when we say the words "I am in recovery"? In the latter there is something that happens to the energy of the word.

As we can see, society uses this term recovery all the time. You recover from an illness, you recover from an accident, you recover from childhood hurts, like the bully at school or the mean teacher, you recover from the death of someone you love. Do you though? Maybe you don't want to go back and hash out all the stuff again, however, there can be unhealthy repetitive behaviors and thoughts that still exist. It's time to uncover what's really at the root of your patterns, addictions, and medicators.

Medicators for us are any coping mechanisms
we use to avoid dealing with our challenges.

Maybe you've tried it all; the support group, the online diet, the yoga flow class, the app on your phone that reminds you to breathe, or how many steps you should be taking per day, you know the deal. You may have tried to go cold turkey. For example, no more cigarettes, no more alcohol, no social media, but something activates you and you are back to where you started.

Here's the deal, Uncovering Your Recovery isn't always going to feel great. It does require action and dedication on your part. Just like recovering from surgery, a cold/flu, or a pandemic; there is going to be discomfort, there might even be pain, but in the end it's definitely worth it. We are going to take this journey together, using all the tools we've learned along the way. We are going to help you uncover your own healing journey to empower your life.

During our friendship together we have traveled a lot of the same paths in the healing world over many years. During this time, we have noticed similarities in ourselves and our clients that made us question everything. We started discussing our own journey of self-healing and found that some things were working, and some things were not. Through our mutual support of each other we came to realize that it's really okay to question everything you've learned in life. It's okay to question your parents, grandparents, society, your friends, the church, your teachers, world leaders, you name it, you get to question it. So we started questioning what it means to recover, and we uncovered a lot of valuable tools which we now share with you in the hopes that you will no longer feel alone and unsupported.

Newsflash: This is For Everyone

Whether you are currently using alcohol, drugs, gambling, scrolling, exercise, work, cigarettes, sex, shopping, eating, or any other distraction, don't stop on account of us. That's not what this is about. This work is designed for you to uncover your **WHY**. We will give you the tools to get curious and aware so you can get to your own truth and possibly change your unhealthy patterns and behaviors.

Maybe after a hectic day at work you come home and have a glass of wine. That doesn't seem like an issue. You don't *think* you're like the drunk family member at the holidays. Maybe you're the bike enthusiast who rides one hundred miles a weekend, but you missed your daughter's recital because you just had to get those last forty miles in. Or you shop only on weekends, but you can't afford what you bought and then the cycle of debt rises, but you keep shopping for the newest thing. Stop for a moment and take a little inventory. Does any of this resonate? Be honest with yourself; it's okay, no one is watching you. We've been there too. We've got your back. You are not alone. It's okay too if you aren't ready to admit it.

You might be reading this and thinking to yourself that you had a great childhood, and your life was pretty awesome compared to others. Your parents were fantastic and supportive and wonderful, and you had everything you ever needed. That's great, no need to read further, right? You're good? We challenge you to stay with us and see what pieces you might uncover in this recovery journey that opens you to a deeper place within yourself.

Every person is eligible to recover from the labels, the stigmas, the scars, the abuse, and all the hurts that living can bring. This book is for you wherever you find yourself. We see you, and we support you. When we face these wounds, we heal ourselves from the inside-out. This work gives us the choice to embrace balance over imbalance, harmony over disharmony, healthy over unhealthy actions.

Maura: For me achieving self-love and self-respect has been a life-long battle, education, and continued challenge. I was not shown, nor given the tools growing up, to understand these concepts. We were taught to always look to improve yourself so the focus was AL-WAYS on what was wrong with us, or how we could do better, or what was missing! Religion taught us to want for nothing, because not only does someone else always have it worse off than you do, but it is also selfish to consider yourSELF in any way at all. That paradigm and belief gets twisted with the whole concept of self-care. If self-care is not modeled for you in your life, how could we ever be expected to practice it on our own?

The following saying is bullshit:

"You can't love anyone else unless you love yourself."

What a bunch of crap!! This is yet another layer to add on top of already feeling "wrong" about so many things! For most of my life I felt near-zero love for myself. Yet I have loved others with a fierceness and a depth no one can challenge.

What I have learned is that self-love needs to be taught, in small steps, in actions, words, behaviors, acceptance, patience, kindness all toward MYSELF! I am only NOW at this age learning how to do that. I believe it will be a life-long study for me. We will all just have to stay tuned to see how I do!

Ann: For me, on this same note, I feel that the way back to learning self-love and self-care is the word Respect. In order for us to learn to love ourselves, we need to find respect for ourselves. Respect is an action word. Respect for self includes boundaries around who we let in our lives to support us. When love has been modeled or taught to us in the form of abuse, manipulation, anger and harm, how would we know what loving ourselves really means?

Through unconditional support and kindness
we can heal by learning to respect ourselves.

Respect can then be transformed into loving ourselves and caring for ourselves more completely. We believe by the time you finish this book, your understanding and awareness of recovery will change.

Journal Entry from Ann

Where did the first steps of recovery start? One night in 1987, that's where. When one person uttered the words out loud to me, "What happened to you when you were a kid was not your fault." The real world slipped away in that moment the surreal became real. Who it was or how it happened isn't important. The message was key. Someone had seen me, knew the secret I had been carrying, and I was now exposed. The events after that led me on my continued path of uncovering my recovery over the past thirty-seven years.

The road has been filled with many twists and turns, sometimes avoiding the debris in the road other times hitting it straight on and getting lost for a while, while picking up shards of my lost self. Nonetheless, the road has led me to this book, this place in supporting others with unconditional love and compassion.

For me, the three essentials I needed on the journey within were love, compassion, and kindness. To be loved and seen without judgment, and to be held with compassion that I am enough. I have found these both from the kindness of others, which then allowed me to find them inside myself. I'm eternally grateful.

Out of the many valuable things I learned along the way, one is the concept of capacity. I still work with this concept every day. Capacity teaches me about compassion. I believe that compassion is an action word. It means I can have compassion for humanity, even people I don't particularly like or who have hurt me. Compassion, especially self-compassion, also means that I no longer need to accept bad behavior from anyone at any time. I've had to learn that others along the road will not always have the same capacity at the same time to heal, to grow, to be self-aware, or to look deeper for more meaning. This has caused me distress countless times because in the past I wanted to fix it and change others like I have changed. I believed that if I could change my whole life and behaviors then anyone could. But I learned my role is not to be a "fixer." Along with other tools, I also use prayer. I pray for myself and others using the Metta prayer. I learned this particular prayer years ago from a small book that I carry with me. It's called A Pocket Full of Miracles, *by Joan Borysenko. It's her version of the Loving Kindness prayer or meditation.*

The Metta Prayer:

May I be at peace, may my heart remain open.
May I awaken to the light of my own true nature.
May I be healed and may I be a source of healing to others.

This practice is profound, and it has changed me. It taught me the invaluable lesson; to be a witness to other people's sadness, pain and grief, without feeling compelled to change or fix it for them, is the most loving thing we can do. To honor them and hold space with unconditional love and support.

My journey continues daily, and my practices shift sometimes from day to day. I'm not always consistent in my "shoulding" of myself. Should is when we tell ourselves repeatedly that we "should" do something. I have chosen to do what works for me, which is to pick up pieces here and there that resonate for me and tuck them in my toolbox of healing things.

I believe that in rigidity there's no space for flow. Flow is the movement that happens even when we are still. I can miss the opportunity for spontaneity and then miss an opportunity for being fully present, which is where we are when we pay full attention in the now of now.

I still have miles to go. I continue looking, observing, listening, and being in this process of life. As long as we are here, there is something else to uncover about ourselves that draws us back to the reflection of the Divine that I believe lives in all of us, by whatever name you call it. I believe we are all born into this vast world at the exact moment we are supposed to be and that our job is to uncover our Light that is already planted inside our hearts from the beginning, which is pure, unconditional loving acceptance of self and others through the superpower of compassion.

The road is not always easy. The pain and suffering we feel along the way can make any mere mortal turn back and hide and take on any other way, through medicating to numbness. Our addictions, compulsions, unhealthy patterns, and unhealthy choices sometimes seem the only way rather than moving through such pain and such suffering. This road of uncovering requires courage and bravery. It requires you starting somewhere and just moving forward. If you're stuck on the road, and you look around, there's usually a path somewhere around you that will lead you out. It's not always the usual path that everyone else follows either. In the words of the poet Robert Frost, "I took the one less traveled and that has made all the difference."

I don't have all the answers for you, I only have the loving compassion of being an unconditional support for you to take the first step. Just like in my beginning when my world became surreal. In an instant that person helped me along the way without judgment. My gratitude is deep.

Let's continue our healing journey together throughout the following pages.

Permission Slip

Please take the time now to fill out this slip for yourself.

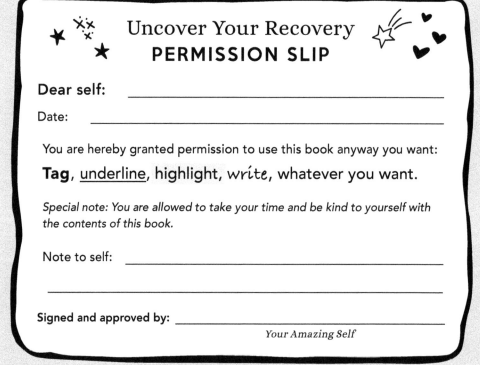

Uncover Your Recovery
PERMISSION SLIP

Dear self: _____

Date: _____

You are hereby granted permission to use this book anyway you want:

Tag, <u>underline</u>, highlight, write, whatever you want.

Special note: You are allowed to take your time and be kind to yourself with the contents of this book.

Note to self: _____

_____

Signed and approved by: _____

Your Amazing Self

Invitation/Challenge

Take advantage of this opportunity: Write something that you found meaningful or significant from this chapter.

Ann's List # BE KIND
to yourself

- [ ] Breathe
- [ ] Sleep, rest, take a nap
- [ ] Drink water
- [ ] Eat nourishing food
- [ ] Take a break from social media
- [ ] Shut off phone
- [ ] Ask for a hug
- [ ] Drink a cup of tea or coffee
- [ ] Watch a funny movie
- [ ] Laugh out loud
- [ ] Spend time in a garden
- [ ] Go to the library
- [ ] Stay in your pj's all day
- [ ] Take a bath or shower
- [ ] Purge old socks and underwear
- [ ] Go for a drive
- [ ] Get fresh air
- [ ] Go to the park
- [ ] Go to the beach
- [ ] Ask for support
- [ ] Go to the mountains
- [ ] Read a book

- [ ] Stretch
- [ ] Watch the sunrise or sunset
- [ ] Light a candle
- [ ] Give yourself a foot massage
- [ ] Have breakfast for dinner
- [ ] Compliment yourself
- [ ] Watch funny animal videos
- [ ] Take yourself out to eat
- [ ] Doodle, color, or draw
- [ ] Sing out loud
- [ ] Listen to birds
- [ ] Go for a bike ride
- [ ] Star gaze
- [ ] Buy a new pillow
- [ ] Buy yourself flowers
- [ ] Go for a walk
- [ ] Watch an old movie
- [ ] Go to a museum
- [ ] Go for a swim
- [ ] Pet a pet
- [ ] Practice gratitude
- [ ] Walk in the rain
- [ ] Get a massage or facial

MAURA'S MESSAGE FROM SPIRIT

The Earth told me a story today.

I am a solid foundation.
Layers of magic.
Soil and dirt.
Crystals and water.
Roots and seeds.
Growth and death.
Vibrant life cycles.
Beauty and rebirth.
Comfort and safety.
Security and strength.
Foundation of life.

You. You are the Earth.

CHAPTER 2

Uncover Your Curiosity and Awareness

"It takes a long time to sift through the more superficial voices of your own gift in order to enter into the deep signature and tonality of your Otherness. When you speak from that deep, inner voice, you are really speaking from the unique tabernacle of your own presence. There is a voice within you that no one, not even you, has ever heard. Give yourself the opportunity of silence and begin to develop your listening in order to hear, deep within yourself, the music of your own spirit."

- JOHN O'DONOHUE
Excerpt from Anam Cara

Curiosity and awareness are vitally important. Being curious, asking yourself questions, and being aware are all key elements of healing. The idea of self-inquiry isn't new, but it can be profound. In the quest for healing or feeling better, this practice is paramount. It requires honesty about our behaviors, good or bad. It invites us to start to listen without judgment, to the still small voice inside of us and can create a different conversation within. Effective self-inquiry requires compassion. As Buddha said, "If your compassion doesn't include yourself it is incomplete." Compassion, kindness, and self-care. We have not easily come by these attributes; we have struggled with being kind and gentle to our own selves. In the past we were taught the tougher we were on ourselves and the more we expected from ourselves, the more successful we would be. That is so far from the truth. The reality is the more compassion we can have for ourselves the faster we can arrive at a place of healing. Little did we know this was the "shortcut" we had been searching for all along.

As we explore our curiosity and awareness we can become clear about what self-inquiry is. In short, it's when you take some time to get honest with yourself about yourself. Self-inquiry requires us to take a full look in the mirror, allowing ourselves to take off any illusions we might be wearing. One definition found on endless-satsang.com states this:

"At first, self-inquiry is just that: IN-quiry. It is a turning of attention and curiosity inwards towards yourself and towards the truth of your nature. It is a practice of redirecting attention away from outward objects, events, and experiences and towards the experiences within your body and being, including subtle experiences within awareness itself. Eventually this inward focus can lead to an experience of your ultimate true nature."

– AUTHOR NIRMALA

The first line of the definition above says it all: "At first, self-inquiry is just that: IN-quiry. It is a turning of attention and curiosity inwards towards yourself and towards the truth of your nature."

The IN part is the key. We spend a lot of time, energy and focus on other people, places, and things, and we forget that we have our own inner thoughts and feelings. It's easy to get distracted. Self-inquiry is a powerful practice. When you use these tools, they can assist you in uncovering your unlimited potential for healing and peace.

Maybe you don't have any questions right now. Your unique story and all of your history makes up who you are now, and how you live your life. When you are given a safe, supportive place to examine and reflect on all of those things, what you uncover will finally help you recover, and heal in ways you didn't know about. If you can look at self-inquiry as an adventure, you give yourself the chance to see things in a new light and from a new perspective. This can make all the difference.

Whatever brought you here to this book, give yourself permission to continue reading and exploring. It might be a great time to get a journal out and start jotting down some notes, or if you are like us, we love to underline and highlight things in books so we can come back to them again and again. Take a deep breath and a long exhale. Allow yourself to think, be curious, be aware, and be open. Let this book guide you and become a friend, a cheerleader, and a support to you as you challenge yourself.

. . . .

Right this second get curious. Stop and think about your family of origin.

Do you buy the same things at the store that they do?
  - Toothpaste, laundry detergent, cereal, toilet paper, etc.

Do you go to the same church?

Watch the same TV shows?

Buy or wear the same brand of clothes?

Buy the same brand of cars?

You get the idea. Ask yourself, what is unique and original that you choose to do apart from your family of origin?

- -

Here are some other questions to ask in the name of self-inquiry:

Were you encouraged when you were young to step outside the family box and try new things?

Was your curiosity something that was supported by your family?

Were your able to explore without constant hovering from a parent?

Were you pushed or felt pressure to do what your parents or family wanted you to do?

Did you do things because you had to or you would suffer the consequences?

Are there now patterns in your life that you can't seem to change?

. . . .

You are not alone. At one time or another, all of us living on the planet have experienced something that has caused us to question ourselves. We may feel stuck, unmotivated, or we can even feel an underlying sadness that we just can't shake. Do you start and stop projects, feeling excited at the onset, and then over time become bored and never finish anything? Ideas pop into our heads, we buy the items to make the projects, and then we put them in a box never to be seen again. Put your hand up if you feel like you've been living on a merry-go-round and can't seem to get off sometimes. Let's do this together. Let's question everything together and at the same time we will find that hidden treasure that will allow us to find the peace we seek even in the chaos. There are answers.

From this moment forth, here is your invitation to ALWAYS BE CURIOUS. We invite you to make curiosity a priority. Start this moment and look at your life, your choices, and your daily ins and outs with a curious and open mind. A mind of wonder, without judgments and criticisms. You can make this a sacred time and a sacred and safe place for you to freely explore. Denial really has no place here. Raw honesty will bring you answers and a peace that you may not have experienced in a very long time, if ever. After all, this is between you and yourself. This is a clean slate.

Using curiosity does have its drawbacks. It isn't an easy practice, and it's not for the faint of heart. When we use curiosity, we can question everything we think about; the way we see things, our whole perception of life. We must pull back the veil of our past and sometimes reframe the things we were taught, the behaviors we came to use and sometimes even our whole value system, in order to heal. It's like realizing that the sky is not blue and that it has a million different hues, and now we can accept that there are many variations on the color of the sky. The breaking of this illusion isn't easy. It's a small step forward with acknowledgement that maybe there's a different shade of blue, and that eases us into a bigger awareness of the multitude of colors that exist.

Think about something in your own life that has been an absolute. Maybe it's a family attribute. Perhaps in your family everyone teases each other. It's a known fact to you and everyone else that your family is a family of teasers. You even laugh about it when the family gets together. One day though you notice that the teasing isn't really teasing, and your feelings get hurt. This is where curiosity gets moving. Your brother always calls you a sissy. You've laughed about it forever, but now you realize it is mean-spirited. Breaking it down, you realize he means you aren't really strong, you aren't really smart, and you are too sensitive. Wow. It takes a lot of courage and bravery to set a boundary around something that you now see as hurtful. Boundaries are discussed further in Chapter 3. In the above situation of teasing, you might need an action step such as, the next time it happens, you step into bravery, find your voice, and tell them how you feel. This is an action step on your part. You can then allow their reactions and possible discomfort to be their responsibility. You've said your part, you put self-respect over being uncomfortable and you no longer allow teasing.

We gave you this example of teasing above. Now take some time for your own curiosity. Maybe you can become aware of something in your past that keeps coming up in your life today. Go back and examine something specific from your family of origin or school days in childhood. Just identify it for now. Can you see it in a different light? Using curiosity you may be able to begin to connect the dots of things that activate you now and their connection to something in your past.

When we are activated, feelings or sensations may arise that feel uncomfortable. We may even feel tense, anxious, or overwhelmed. This activation is also called a trigger. When this happens it can cause strong reactions or emotions to come up.

> *Being activated by something is a*
> *natural occurrence which happens to all of us.*

How we respond to these activations can change over time when we start to have more curiosity about our sensations in our body.

During this amazing process there is no need to be less than truthful with yourself. There is no one grading you on this process. It is not a test. It is a powerful healing experience. Denial and pretending that everything is okay leads to suffering. The more we repress our truths, our feelings and our reality, the more damage we can cause ourselves, and even others as well. This can be the most private and intimate experience you can work on. Unless you want to, you do not have to share this journey with anyone else. Of course, we recommend you reach out for support at some point as an opportunity to build a system of healthy foundations. Those new foundations can aid your long-term success. But if you feel the need to begin this process alone, we understand the need for you to protect your privacy. Lean into your own confidentiality. Set the intention to work without self-judgment and with truth. When you create this safe and sacred space for yourself, you will discover a peace that you have not experienced before. This is only the beginning.

Personal Story from Maura

When my mother was diagnosed with lung cancer, it rocked the foundation of our family. She had surgery to remove her lung, and they believed they had gotten all the cancer. We were hopeful. Less than two years later when the cancer was discovered in her other lung, they told us she had six months to a year to live. Six weeks later, in April of 2002, thirteen days before my thirty-seventh birthday, my mother died.

It was beyond devastating. The grief was so deep that between April and August that year I was physically ill. I had walking pneumonia; I was struggling with severe depression. I was completely disconnected from my life. There was nothing left of me. I was hollow and empty inside. My light had gone out. If there was ever a time for self-inquiry, this was it. That August, I finally found myself in a therapist's office. Little did either of us know, we would embark on a seven-year journey together that would change me forever and save my life.

I still owe my therapist, Lisa Leidecker, a debt of gratitude I can never repay.

As a standard practice with someone in my condition and state of mind, I was sent off to be evaluated by a psychiatrist. Over the next two or three years a few different diagnoses were brought up and discussed. Different medications were prescribed and tried. Mood Disorder? Anxiety? Major Depressive Disorder? Bipolar? There were some interesting complications in figuring out the "category" I best fit into. Why, you ask? Hmmm. Well, that itself was an interesting uncovering.

Not at all funny at the time, but now I can look back and feel so sorry for all those who had to deal with me then. They certainly had their hands full. My Spiritual Gifts were developing rapidly at that time. I was led to seek out answers to better understand this concept of DEATH. Inquire, inquire, inquire! I mean seriously, where WAS my mother?! I thought, "She would never really leave me." I was searching and searching. As we all do when we are suffering a deep loss, we search for relief from our grief. My heart was completely broken. And so, I embarked on what would become the discovery of my next purpose in this life, this Spiritual Oasis. It opened a world of doors and universes to me that I didn't realize existed. And the first thing I studied in this new world was Mediumship.

Mediumship, if you don't know, is the connecting to and communicating with someone in the Spirit World, someone who has passed on. It is a communication between the living and the dead. Now for those that do not believe, I get it. It is not what most of us grew up with. In fact, it is considered sinful in some religions. I was raised Roman Catholic. My mother worked at the church! So, I know all too well how it is viewed. And believe me, some of my family members still remind me. There was a certain amount of discomfort in my pursuing this interest. But understand this, I had to find my mother. I had to connect with her. After all, WHERE was she? My religious upbringing was limiting that scope. As strong as my faith was that she was with God, and in Heaven, I still needed more.

I began classes and workshops in the Fall of 2002. Almost immediately, and because God led me to the most talented and gifted teachers and practitioners, I began communicating with Spirit. I strengthened and developed my intuition. I went on to learn how to Channel the Angels. I took all kinds of classes. I conducted all types of Readings. I had all kinds of wonderful, crazy, happy, and painful experiences. But the thing is this, HOW can you properly diagnose someone who . . . yep, "HEARS VOICES?" That was a difficult thing to figure out. For them, and for me.

I was changing so much. One of the important things I learned is that it is completely inappropriate to read someone without their permission. But in my early and not-yet-trained days, I did not understand the ethics of this. I would just blurt things out. Almost anywhere. Things that I later understood had accurately come from Spirit. But at the time, I was so uneducated about it all. Sharing personal, private information without consideration of another person's beliefs, feelings, surroundings & environment, is not okay. Without their consent, *you do not share such things with therapists, psychiatrists, medical doctors, and their personnel, strangers, or at bars, parties, public settings, etc. There is a proper time and place. Readings contain sacred, private information that needs to be exchanged in secure and trusted environments with the utmost privacy and consideration. Over the years I had to learn the reverence of this work. But at the time of these missteps twenty-two years ago, can you imagine the confusion it caused? Like, sharing with someone that their significant other is being unfaithful, or telling your dentist that he needs to get his heart checked out as soon as possible, or mentioning to your new doctor that their Grandmother has a message for them. In defense of the professionals, I wouldn't know how to properly diagnose me either. I wonder if there are any books out there on that topic! Like:* How can Spirituality blend well with diagnosis and psychiatry. *(HA!)*

In the meantime, I was sure learning a lot about myself, and the biggest thing that kept me going throughout all the pain was my curiosity. What about you? Are you a naturally curious person like me? This is a good time to start asking yourself that and actively begin exploring the superpower of curiosity. It continues to open up so many new worlds for me, and it will do the same for you. We have a lot to unpack. Stay on this journey with us. As you step deeper inside of yourself our hope is that we take the rest of this ride together.

♡ Journal Entry from Ann

If you find me not approachable,
Can you look inside yourself and see if the same resides there?
Are you approachable, do you allow others into your space?

If you find me bossy,
Can you look inside yourself and see where that might resonate?
Is it really a bossiness you feel from me, or could it be confidence, empowerment?

If you find me distracted,
Can you look inside at your own busyness and see if it might be your reflection in me?

If you find me to be angry or mad,
Can you look inside yourself and see what anger lies at the edge of your own field?
Are you activated by your perception of my anger, or are you actually angry and don't know what to do with it?

If you find me funny,
Can you look inside yourself and find your own humor, your own joy if you think you don't have such abilities?

If you find me too talkative,
Can you be still for a moment and look inside and see if you are talking too much and not listening with purpose?

If you find me loving,
Can you look inside yourself and notice your own loving heart? Is it open or is it closed? Is the vulnerability too much? What can you notice about the way you love?

If you find me hard to understand,
Can you take a look inside your own understanding and see if you are communicating in a way that is loving and kind or in some other way that does not serve?

If you find me kind,
Can you look at your own kindness, the way you give to others, the way you think of others, are you too giving, too kind where you have nothing left for yourself?

If you find me out of touch,
Can you find ways that you are out of touch, can you read more, engage more with the world around you? Knowledge is power. What have you been reading or engaging with your mind?

What can you be curious about in your reflection of how you respond to others? Observe, reflect, allow, be honest. Awareness can come from a variety of sources. We can start by asking ourselves, "What Do I need?"

Permission Slip

Please take the time now to fill out this slip for yourself.

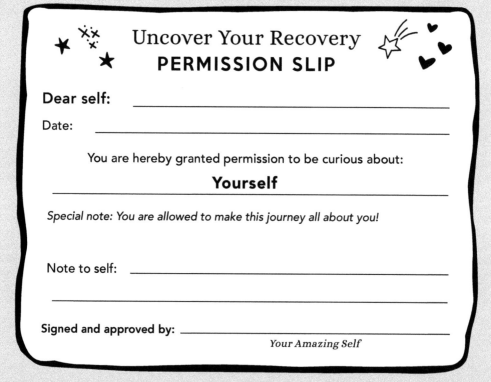

Uncover Your Recovery
PERMISSION SLIP

Dear self: _____

Date: _____

You are hereby granted permission to be curious about:

Yourself
_____

Special note: You are allowed to make this journey all about you!

Note to self: _____

_____

Signed and approved by: _____

Your Amazing Self

Invitation/Challenge

Take advantage of this opportunity: Write something that you found meaningful or significant from this chapter.

BE KIND
to yourself

- [ ] Breathe
- [ ] Sleep, rest, take a nap
- [ ] Drink water
- [ ] Eat nourishing food
- [ ] Take a break from social media
- [ ] Shut off phone
- [ ] Ask for a hug
- [ ] Drink a cup of tea or coffee
- [ ] Watch a funny movie
- [ ] Laugh out loud
- [ ] Spend time in a garden
- [ ] Go to the library
- [ ] Stay in your pj's all day
- [ ] Take a bath or shower
- [ ] Purge old socks and underwear
- [ ] Go for a drive
- [ ] Get fresh air
- [ ] Go to the park
- [ ] Go to the beach
- [ ] Ask for support
- [ ] Go to the mountains
- [ ] Read a book

- [ ] Stretch
- [ ] Watch the sunrise or sunset
- [ ] Light a candle
- [ ] Give yourself a foot massage
- [ ] Have breakfast for dinner
- [ ] Compliment yourself
- [ ] Watch funny animal videos
- [ ] Take yourself out to eat
- [ ] Doodle, color, or draw
- [ ] Sing out loud
- [ ] Listen to birds
- [ ] Go for a bike ride
- [ ] Star gaze
- [ ] Buy a new pillow
- [ ] Buy yourself flowers
- [ ] Go for a walk
- [ ] Watch an old movie
- [ ] Go to a museum
- [ ] Go for a swim
- [ ] Pet a pet
- [ ] Practice gratitude
- [ ] Walk in the rain
- [ ] Get a massage or facial

MAURA'S MESSAGE FROM SPIRIT

Spider told me a story today.

Build your beautiful Web
Made of finest silk and intricate Divine Design
Catching all that comes to you
Leaving behind all you do not need
Move on to create your next piece
Life is like that
Your life
Create, weave, attract
Leave what no longer serves you
Go Create new Masterpieces
Over and over
They are each unique, beautiful, powerful
A Mystical Design from Above

You. You are a Web Maker.

CHAPTER 3

Uncover Your Truth

"Our deepest fear is not that we are inadequate. Our deepest fear is that we are powerful beyond measure. It is our light, not our darkness that most frightens us. We ask ourselves, 'Who am I to be brilliant, gorgeous, talented, fabulous?' Actually, who are you not to be? You are a child of God. Your playing small does not serve the world."

- MARIANNE WILLIAMSON
A Return to Love: Reflections on the Principles of "A Course in Miracles"

If you feel like taking a deep breath before we dive into this chapter go right ahead because thinking about the word "truth" sometimes can make us feel uncomfortable and we understand that. This is the truth about uncovering what is *your truth,* not the truth of the world, not the truth about what other people think, but ***your own personal truth***. Take that deep breath and exhale now, we'll wait.

So where do we start? Well with truth, yes, but the truth of what? All the stuff we have ever been told about good or bad, right and wrong, girls are weak and boys are strong has just been a setup. Is any of that the truth? We have been labeled since the beginning without our permission.

If we had come into a family that revered both girls and boys for their intrinsic value as human beings, and not based on gender, we might all feel differently about ourselves. Perhaps then we would hold the belief that we are all created equal. Although we do believe the younger generation is changing this, most of us did not come from families that honor that truth.

It is not lost on us that this change is ripe to happen now considering the gender issues facing young people today. A perfect example is the way that the younger generation is using their own labels to identify themselves, i.e., they/them, he/him, she/her. Some of the older generation does not get it. Some get fearful and uncomfortable and have a lack of tolerance for this new way of thinking. It challenges their whole system of beliefs, labels, and truths.

Another example of the way truth is unfolding is that a generation of people have been questioning their strict religious values now. Some have stopped going to organized church, some have stopped any kind of religious beliefs at all. This new generation has permission now to question everything, in order to find their own truth.

We all have labels that have been given to us or that we picked up over the years, and not just the general labels of "daughter" or "son" or "parent" or "student." We have other labels that we tend to own or believe to be our truth, that really don't belong to us.

For example, if you're labeled the "smart one" does that mean that you're not the "funny one"?

If you're labeled the "sensitive one," does that mean you aren't brave?

What if you were labeled fat, or skinny or some other body identification, how did this define you?

What if you exuded confidence and were labeled bossy?

What if you were quiet and were labeled weird?

We're inviting you, as you learned in the last chapter, to get curious, use self-inquiry, and gain awareness. When you start asking who you are through the lens of truth, your choice of luggage changes and you get to now pack your own bags.

It's important that we start to uncover these places of truth in ourselves so we can look at our behaviors and why we choose the ones we do. At this point we don't have to change anything we are doing, but instead give ourselves permission to be curious about what our truth is and how it affects our current behaviors as it relates to the topic of Uncovering Your Recovery and Healing. We can unpack all the bags and labels and look at them with a fresh view and choose which labels we will keep and carry going forward, and which ones we will discard and leave behind. We will create space in our unique bags for new and healthy things we pick up along our journey of self-discovery.

We repeat this a lot in the book, doing this work takes great courage and bravery. Let's face it, it takes courage to stand up and look at our family's histories, their shortcomings, their lack of knowledge, and their lack of awareness. We want to truly believe that our families have our best interests at heart. But they are human; they come with their own faulty wiring through the generations. We are currently living in a time when it's okay to release our families of origin and any accompanying generational wounding. Right now, in this present time we have more freedom than the generation before us to expand, to explore, to gain more knowledge and awareness, and to use our curiosity. As we continue to uncover our truth, we also start the work of our deep healing. And this gives us permission to take personal responsibility for all our current choices, actions, and behaviors.

Personal Boundaries and Perceptions

This is a great time to discuss the concept of personal boundaries. Personal boundaries are the limits and rules we set for ourselves as they relate to our connection to other people. As our healing increases, the limits we set with others define what we find acceptable or unacceptable in their behavior toward us. Some important healthy boundaries include keeping ourselves safe, communicating our needs, and saying no when necessary. All too often we accept responsibility for the emotional responses of others, overlooking our own needs. Our needs matter. We may have not learned about these healthy boundaries in our families of origin. We have an invitation now in uncovering our truth to review them, change them and reset them as needed or maybe even for the first time. If setting boundaries is new to you be mindful that this will likely be uncomfortable for you and others. When we have unhealthy or weak boundaries we tend to be taken advantage of sometimes without our awareness. People might get used to us always saying yes or being agreeable. When we establish new boundaries, there can be resistance and it can bring up anger in others. As we previously mentioned, other people's emotional responses to our setting boundaries is not our responsibility. It might be time to stop compromising. When you say no to others, you are saying yes to yourself. This is powerful.

When we are examining and uncovering our truths we need to also consider our perceptions. Perceptions are stories that we create from our personal, lived experiences. When we continue to stay in our perceptions without challenging them, we create a barrier to our healing.

We set up stories to protect ourselves.

It takes courage to look inside and examine our perceptions of people and situations. When we do take the time for this examination, we can use the tools of curiosity and awareness to help us see differently.

Perceptions are unique to our own personal experiences. No two people experience the same situation in the same way. This is because the lens in which we view life has been molded by our family, society, culture, school, religion, karma, past lives, etc. Perceptions sometimes get clouded because we see them as truth or fact, and this might not be entirely accurate. Individual truths can be multifaceted. Perceptions can be changed through curiosity, awareness, and self-inquiry.

For example, a cultural perception is that women are supposed to be homemakers. Although this is an old perception there are a lot of people that still hold this belief. In your family of origin, what is your perception of this? Was this idea of women being homemakers something that you perceived to be true of women? Did anyone else in your family believe this to be truth? What is your perception of this now? Be honest.

Another cultural perception is that females can't do traditionally "male" jobs. Again, this is an old perception and it's changing. What is your perception of this view? What was your family's perception of jobs concerning gender?

Another concept that ties into our truths and perceptions is the idea of "Should"-ing. Seems like everyone wants to "should" on us, especially ourselves. Do you ever hear yourself say I should do this, or I should do that? Where does this original thought of should come from? The world is full of "shoulds." Stop and think about it for a minute. Think of all the times you hear your own self say, "I should." This is an opportunity to use curiosity and awareness to examine the self "should"-ing. There's so much pressure in the word "should" and it can create undo anxiety and stress. It might seem funny, this concept of "should"-ing but when we release ourselves from this damaging perceived obligation, we create so much relief and so much room for healing.

Let's remember that our truths, shoulds, boundaries, and perceptions need to be challenged with curiosity, awareness, and compassion for our continued growth.

Journal Entry from Ann

Ever wonder about truth? Like what it is and if there really is any sort of thing as truth? I've wondered about this a lot. I have a lot of truths that are based in reality.

My name is Ann, I live in a house in the woods with my husband.

My family lives around me. I have a car.

I love pizza.

I've been a lover of the color purple my whole life.

Are these truths or facts? Are they the same? Don't we use the two interchangeably most of the time. We say the "Truth is," "The Fact of the matter is," but who determines what's true and what's a fact? Wow, how far down the rabbit hole we could wander with this idea. So, let's rein it in a bit. Let's look at truth from the idea of family beliefs, values, and perceptions and how it relates to our journey of Uncovering our Recovery.

Let's use the story of you coming into the world. Just imagine in the beginning before you got here, you packed two bags full of love, light, excitement, joy, and adventure. Filling up most of your bags though was love, pure unconditional love, and joy. It was your gift, tucked in the center of your heart for safekeeping, that you received from the Universe to take with you on your journey. You were excited to get here. You had no idea why you were actually coming on this particular trip, whether the people that were waiting for you were happy or sad that you were arriving; you just knew that your bags were packed because it was your time.

You arrived! Let's imagine though, for this scenario, when you got here things were good when you arrived. People were excited that you were here, they held you, carried you around, fed you, diapered you, and kept you safe. All was right with the world. Your trip had begun just right. You had your bags packed for your two little hands and you were happy.

As you started moving farther into your journey you realized you had an extra bag or two that you didn't bring with you. You didn't question the bags, but you noticed them and kept them with you. Every time your birthday rolled around there was a new bag with you. You weren't really sure what to do with them just yet, but you kept carrying them around. As you got a little older and started to understand life a little better, you started peeking in the bags to find out what was inside. Some of it you didn't understand; some of the things seemed odd to you.

There were things in the bags marked with words and sayings like, "attitudes and opinions," and others were labeled, "you can do better," or "you don't measure up." Some even said "sadness" "anger" and "resentment" on them. Some bags had names on them too, like "Mom's bag" or "Dad's bag," or teacher, coach, etc. Digging deeper still, you saw even more stuffed into the corner of the bags, these had bigger labels on them, like fat, ugly, sissy, weird, and stupid. You were confused, but you kept the bags anyway, along with your own, because it's what you had always done: Kept the bags.

This is also where mixed messages can come in when actions and words don't match. Since our parents/caregivers influence our truth during our upbringing, our truth can get buried in the confusion of words that are spoken and unspoken and actions that are taken. Children can inherently read the energy in the room. When you were a kid, if your parents were saying one thing and their actions were saying another, you noticed the inconsistency. We are left now to figure out what the truth really is for ourselves. Is it our actions that speak from our truth now or is it our words?

Right now, can you stop and think about this idea for a minute? You came in pure with love and light tucked in your heart from the Universe. Then without your permission, other people started piling their stuff into your life and giving you their bags to carry around as well. Can you be curious for a second and really let that sink in? You have been carrying around stuff with you that's not yours for a really, really long time. It's okay now to examine what is yours and what is yours to release.

Identify Current Truths

Looking at the journal entry above can you identify any current truths that you are questioning at this point in your life?

. . . .

What "shoulds" can you shed right now that are coming from someone else and not your own voice?

I should go back to school.

I should get a better job.

I should be a better parent, friend, spouse, partner.

I should de-clutter all the rooms in my house.

You get the idea. Pick something that you "should" yourself about currently.

What bags and labels can you start to unpack and let go of?

I'm not good enough.

I'm not as smart as my sibling.

I'm too fat, too skinny, too bossy.

I'm too sensitive.

I've always been the weird one in the family.

I never seem to fit in.

. . . .

Speak the truth even if your voice shakes.
- MAGGIE KUHN

Permission Slip

Please take the time now to fill out this slip for yourself.

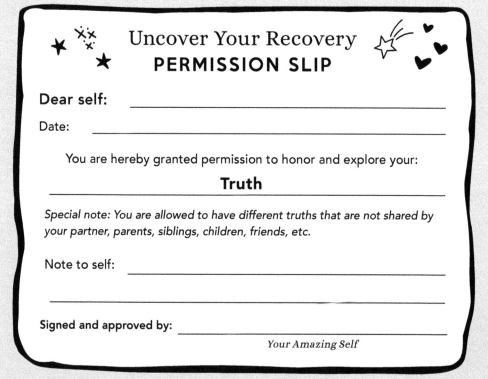

Uncover Your Recovery
PERMISSION SLIP

Dear self: _____

Date: _____

You are hereby granted permission to honor and explore your:

Truth
_____

Special note: You are allowed to have different truths that are not shared by your partner, parents, siblings, children, friends, etc.

Note to self: _____

_____

Signed and approved by: _____

Your Amazing Self

Invitation/Challenge

Take advantage of this opportunity: Write something that you found meaningful or significant from this chapter.

BE KIND
to yourself

- [ ] Breathe
- [ ] Sleep, rest, take a nap
- [ ] Drink water
- [ ] Eat nourishing food
- [ ] Take a break from social media
- [ ] Shut off phone
- [ ] Ask for a hug
- [ ] Drink a cup of tea or coffee
- [ ] Watch a funny movie
- [ ] Laugh out loud
- [ ] Spend time in a garden
- [ ] Go to the library
- [ ] Stay in your pj's all day
- [ ] Take a bath or shower
- [ ] Purge old socks and underwear
- [ ] Go for a drive
- [ ] Get fresh air
- [ ] Go to the park
- [ ] Go to the beach
- [ ] Ask for support
- [ ] Go to the mountains
- [ ] Read a book

- [ ] Stretch
- [ ] Watch the sunrise or sunset
- [ ] Light a candle
- [ ] Give yourself a foot massage
- [ ] Have breakfast for dinner
- [ ] Compliment yourself
- [ ] Watch funny animal videos
- [ ] Take yourself out to eat
- [ ] Doodle, color, or draw
- [ ] Sing out loud
- [ ] Listen to birds
- [ ] Go for a bike ride
- [ ] Star gaze
- [ ] Buy a new pillow
- [ ] Buy yourself flowers
- [ ] Go for a walk
- [ ] Watch an old movie
- [ ] Go to a museum
- [ ] Go for a swim
- [ ] Pet a pet
- [ ] Practice gratitude
- [ ] Walk in the rain
- [ ] Get a massage or facial

Maura's List

BE KIND
to yourself

Watch the sunrise or sunset

Take a break from social media

Doodle, color, or draw

Ask for a hug

Give yourself a foot massage

Compliment yourself

Go to a library

Go for a drive

Stretch

Go for a bike ride

Have breakfast for dinner

Stay in your pj's all day

Take yourself out to eat

Sing out loud

Go to a museum

Star gaze

Listen to music

Practice gratitude

Sleep, rest, take a nap

Light a candle

Watch a funny movie

Shut off phone

Pet a pet

Buy a new pillow

Drink a cup of coffee or tea

Walk in the rain

Go for a swim

Purge old socks and underwear

Take a bath or shower

Listen to birds

Eat nourishing food

Breathe

Watch funny animal videos

Read a book

Get a massage or facial

Laugh out loud

Go to the mountains

Buy yourself flowers

Go for a walk

Ask for support

Get fresh air

Go to the beach

Watch an old movie

Spend time in a garden

Kindness is necessary
when abandonment has been experienced

Abandonment

This Page Left Intentionally Blank

A WORD ABOUT ABANDONMENT

Abandonment is a topic that truly affects so many of us. It can create feelings of disconnection, rejection and even harm.

Once upon a time, we decided to hold a class about abandonment, most especially because it has certainly impacted our lives so deeply. So much so, that we actually abandoned the abandonment class, and never held it.

We found humor in this so often, yet it has been such a great lesson for us. We share this story all the time.

There are many resources, books, blogs, and help available regarding abandonment issues. We aren't going to be covering them in this book. But we are aware it is connected to many deep, personal wounding traumas.

MAURA'S MESSAGE FROM SPIRIT

The Trees told me a story today.

If you were a Tree you'd realize...
When you take on all the sadness and emotions that you feel,
when you keep them all to yourself,
you wither away and slowly die,
getting weaker and weaker,
little by little,
branch by branch,
leaf by leaf,
root by root.

But, if you shared those feelings with all the other Trees that exist,
you would realize that Trees come together
to absorb and share those emotions.
The more Trees, the more sharing.
The more sharing,
the less pain for one lone Tree.

Do not keep the sadness to yourself.
Share it.
Sharing makes you bigger,
and stronger,
and healthier.

You. You are a Tree.

CHAPTER 4

Uncover Your Emotions

*"Someone I loved once gave me a box full of darkness.
It took me years to understand this too was a gift."*

- MARY OLIVER

When we begin to process emotions, there's always a chance we can be taken to the deepest level of recovery. This is an opportunity to listen to the wisdom of your Soul. Emotions and feelings can be a scary place to explore. Whatever our conditioning as children, there's a whole lot of complications that come with being a human that feels. What most of us do though is think. We think and think and think. A wise teacher once said that if we were going to change all our bad habits by thinking about them, we would have changed them already and we wouldn't be in these places of discomfort. Sadly, most people think about their emotions and never actually have access or a capacity to feel them.

We can use our own innate ability to connect to our emotions. There are no special gifts or talents needed. A willingness and awareness can be a doorway to our emotions.

How Do We Access Our Emotions?

Our emotions aren't accessed by thinking about them. Sure, you can think about love, but to actually feel love you have to tune in to a deeper place in your body, not your mind. For anger, you might know you're angry, because sometimes you feel it in your body, like heat, or your face gets flushed, or you make fists. As for happiness, you can think a happy thought, but when you are feeling happy in your body, your mouth smiles, you feel warm inside, you may feel good, and your vibration changes. Therefore, to access these emotions we have to get into our bodies. For a lot of us doing this type of work, the sensations of our bodies are not always comfortable or accessible. It can be challenging to allow yourself to become vulnerable and feel certain emotions. With vulnerability we can sometimes feel unsafe. With support and tools, accessing your emotions and feelings is worth the work it might take to get there.

Let's go back to thinking and feeling and get clear about this idea. We are made up of our body, mind, and spirit. Some might debate the last one, but we believe all three things are needed to make us whole. We will discuss this more in a later chapter.

The first emotion we are going to discuss is anger. Most of us are familiar with this emotion. When we think about being mad, the body reacts as well. When you are feeling angry, you don't just think you are angry, you know you are angry. You might feel tense, want to scream, or you might feel your jaw get tight, your fists might clench, your face might scowl, and your breathing can change. You might even want to run away. There is a multitude of ways we might feel or sense anger. Start to get curious about how you feel about anger. This emotion is rarely discussed with kindness and compassion. Anger is a healthy emotion. It is our body's innate response to protecting ourselves and keeping us safe.

Let's now go back to our family of origin again to check out the ways we were taught to deal with our emotions. Were you allowed to openly express your emotions? All of them, the whole range? Not just happy and sad, but disappointment, resentment, jealousy, vulnerability, fear, confusion? The range of emotions is wide and vast. For example, mad can be annoyance, irritation, exasperation, frustration, etc. Most of us did not grow up having the tools that are available today. For example, the author Diane Alber has written children's books that help children identify and manage emotions. Her work also helps explain tough topics to kids in a fun and interactive way. She became inspired to start writing and illustrating books to support both parents and educators as well, in order to give them an opportunity to provide focus on social-emotional topics such as kindness, empathy, anxiety, and anger. Additionally, the movie *Inside Out* does a great job at introducing feelings and emotions to both children and adults. Nowadays children may have some better tools to access their emotions than we ever had before, but we all need to continuoulsy educate ourselves about how the body, mind, and spirit process emotions.

The healthy way to access emotions is through self-inquiry in a safe and loving environment. Most of the time we didn't have access to this form of support, so we pushed our emotions and feelings aside or buried them. We also could have been overly emotional and demonstrative in our acting out, and this brought us attention, whether it be negative or positive. There needs to be balance. But before that we first must be able to identify the emotions, allow ourselves to feel them, honor them, and give them a voice and a pathway of movement.

If you are stuck and unable to feel your emotions, you probably have dealt with this by using any form of medicator that suited you or suits you still. For instance, if you weren't allowed to be angry in your family home, and if you did express anger, you were yelled at, sent to your room, denied your feelings, or you had no voice, this resulted in having no outlet for your anger. This is how we start to suppress our emotions. Let's be clear, your anger was probably an appropriate response to something or someone, or you wouldn't have felt it in the first place. All our emotions are valid, every single one of them. It's how we process them and deal with them that's important.

When emotions build up over time and get shut down, you might start to reach for something to make you feel better. An unhealthy outlet or escape may start to emerge. Maybe it's alcohol, food, gaming, shopping, getting high, etc. It's rarely ever the positive emotions that we aren't allowed to feel, it's usually the emotions that make other people feel uncomfortable that we haven't been allowed to express. Invariably we are going to try to make others happy because ultimately what we want is to be loved and accepted and feel like we belong. We even deny our feelings and put on a happy face despite our sadness, anger, and disappointment so that other people can feel comfortable. This is a denial of our own truth.

Denial of our emotions is denying our very essence.

This is the piece that needs uncovering so we can heal the core wounding of our hearts. Before we move on, stop for a moment and think about what might be a medicator for you. What might be something that you can be curious about that you use to escape instead of allowing yourself to feel your emotions?

Many of us have been in denial of our emotions for a long time and have no idea what we feel. Accessing these feelings can be overwhelming and uncomfortable. This is a great time to have your resources lined up. Friends on speed dial, making a therapist aware that you are diving in a little deeper, support groups at the ready, hotlines on standby, and showing yourself kindness and gentleness the best you can. Going into this territory could possibly get rocky.

Identifying Emotions

Can you identify your more complex emotions? Can you pick them out from the usual ones like anger, happiness, sadness? There's a plethora of emotions all with their own unique undercoat. One way to identify them is to look at some pictures that express emotions. There are so many photos on the web that can help you identify how you are feeling. If your intellectual awareness is pretty high, but your connection to your body is not, this is where walking the tightrope of emotions and feelings can get confusing.

You might think you are angry, but anger is not in your head, it's in your body. The idea of anger is in your head, but the emotion of anger resides in your body, your tissues, your very cells. This aspect of emotions is hardly ever taught to us by our family, society, or our culture. We have been duped in so many ways into thinking that our mind can get us out of everything. It can't. Yes, the mind is powerful, but remember the body, mind, and spirit are all working in conjunction with each other and are not separate.

Society and our culture would have us believe that we can think our way out of everything. Sometimes we can think our way out of things, yes. But our emotions are a whole other story. For example, if you are grief-filled and you are crying, talking yourself out of crying rarely ever works. You are expressing your sadness physically through your tears, your sobs, through the liquid leaking from your eyes. This is not in your head; it is in your body.

We have to make these connections of body sensations to our emotions in order to identify them and access them. This is a powerful connection to make. Our minds can talk us into and out of anything. We can even go to therapy and tell our therapists exactly what they want to hear. We can convince them and anyone else that we are okay. Funny, though, the body knows the score. When you are sad you can say you are okay, even convince yourself you are, but your body, your tissues, your cells know better. Your body is hard at work responding. Whatever emotion you are feeling, your hormones and other chemicals in your body are involved. Our nervous system, our brain, and our basic body functions are all involved. It is all connected.

What Do We Do With These Emotions?

Once we start to feel these emotions, what do we do with the anger that wells up, the sadness that creates the lump in the throat, or the annoyances that won't stop? Well, we feel them. That's right. We just go ahead and feel them, with all the uncomfortable sensations that show up. We told you this work might be uncomfortable. Healing is challenging work. Think about this, when you are happy or laughing it ebbs and flows. Anger or unpleasant emotions can be the same, they ebb and flow. Stopping them or trying to stop feeling them is not being kind to yourself and is ultimately unhealthy.

In identifying our emotions, we can use some basic natural approaches. We can use our senses to get in touch with and access our emotions. For example, you can use the sense of smell or taste to remind you of something either happy or sad. You can use your sense of hearing and sight, like watching a funny movie or listening to favorite music. The senses help us conjure up memories stored in our bodies. The mind remembers the event, the body reacts with a feeling or a sensation. You eat tomato sauce that reminds you of your Nonna's cooking and you feel a warm sensation of contentment of the memory. On the flip side, you smell a certain perfume, and you are immediately reminded of someone you dated that treated you terribly and you may feel annoyed. You see children playing and you feel happy. You hear them being too loud and you feel grouchy. You listen to old songs that conjure up feelings of nostalgia, or other songs that evoke strong emotions that can move you to joy or even tears. This is mind and body working together.

Maura: When I was nine-years-old, my mom took me to Weight Watchers. Someone in charge of the scale yelled out my weight across a room full of people. The negative attention created such shame and embarrassment that I suppressed these emotions for a good portion of my life. This and other similar contributing factors created a deep wounding that needed to be dissected emotionally, physically, and spiritually. But if I never processed the initial wounding and emotions, the healing would prove difficult to come by. We will go deeper into this healing journey a little later.

Feelings can be truly unpleasant. We spend a lot of time trying to avoid feeling for that reason. Ever wonder why the pharmaceutical business is making money hand over fist at our expense? We never want to feel anything. We take this pill to stop this feeling, we take that pill to stop that feeling. Ever stop and think what medicine actually cures? Antibiotics cure stuff, much of the rest just bandages it up. We need to go into the deep wound, clean it from the inside out, not the outside in. Those first wounds of the body, mind, and spirit never truly disappear, they just become buried in our tissues and cells, and both the body and the mind hold them. Medications can help soothe them, but medication does not cure them.

Let's be clear we are not knocking medication; we are asking you to get curious about it. This is a great time to take an inventory of whatever you are using to numb your emotions.

Don't ever stop taking your prescribed medication. Be curious, do your research, reach out, get help, question everything to make an informed decision that is right for you.

Maura: After being diagnosed with depression and insomnia, I was prescribed medication. I have been on medication for almost twenty years. It has saved my life. It is only one of the tools of my recovery and health program, but it was a difficult decision to accept. My father saw needing medication as a weakness. It took me some time to develop my own beliefs around this, and I am grateful for the support and clarity medication provides. We still need to learn additional tools to deal with our emotions, but this is one option that has been vital for me personally.

We are asking what to do with our emotions once we uncover them. We actually need to feel them, express them, and move them out in healthy ways in order to process them. We can reach out and ask others for help. We can speak up and use our voices to communicate our feelings. We can sing, dance, exercise, paint, draw, doodle, go for a walk, shake our bodies. We can also use alternative methods such as massage, acupuncture, Reiki, etc. **Emotions need movement to finish their expression**. Any expression of an emotion that got stopped in the first place needs to be completed.

For example, if you got angry and were not able to express that anger, you never did get to finish that emotional reaction in your body. It froze. This might be a new concept. That's okay. I don't think any of us were raised in a house that had an "anger room" down the hall or the "sad room" upstairs. Awesome little rooms, furnished with a punching bag, or an art wall, or lots of pillows with soundproofing so you could cry, or yell or scream. That would have been great, right? Imagine in this scenario you would get sent to the anger room, where you would get to yell, paint, draw, sing, and express your emotions in many ways. Whew. You moved it all out. The emotions and feelings got to finish what they started. If only this scenario was the case for all of us, the world would be a much better and healthier place. Our emotions and feelings need to finish. We need to be able to express them in safe and healthy ways. When we are conditioned not to feel or express emotions this creates unhealthy behavior patterns that we may or may not be familiar with.

Many emotions affect our lives
whether we are aware of them or not.

Three of the major contributors to dysfunction, addiction, and unhappiness are shame, blame, and guilt. We are pointing these out specifically because of their catastrophic influences on our healing. You may be judging yourself for past mistakes, choices you have made, things you are even currently still doing. This self-criticism and/or lack of acceptance can be damaging to your emotional self. It takes great courage and bravery to look at the truth and the origin of shame, blame, and guilt. Doing this with love and compassion is the most powerful and kindest way to create lasting healing.

Shame, blame, and guilt are multilayered and may be feelings that have been buried for a very long time. When we can identify them, we can use curiosity as a way in to examine them. Curiosity can lead us out of the darkness of suffering and into the light of wholeness in body, mind, and spirit. It's not your fault when you don't yet have awareness around these emotions. As Maya Angelou once said, "Do the best you can, until you know better. Then when you know better, do better." Once we become aware we can take action and responsibility for our healing.

Shame is defined as a painful feeling of humiliation or distress. Shame is a normal human emotion and when dealt with appropriately it can help us grow. Healthy shame can guide us toward self-correction. Toxic shame is a debilitating feeling of worthlessness and self-loathing that you turn into a harmful belief about yourself. It can start to contaminate the way you see yourself and have you question your self-worth and identity. Toxic shame can have us feel as though we are fundamentally flawed and inadequate, and we can start to believe we are unworthy of love.

Shame can be insidious.

It is possible to carry shame and not be fully aware of it. For example, shame that is not always apparent can stem from relationships. We cannot control who we fall in love with. Think of the following scenarios, relationships of mixed religions, mixed race, or mixed gender. Relationships involving those who are disproportionate in age, such as dating someone much younger or much older than you, relationships involving someone who is married, or otherwise spoken for, etc. If you come from a family that frowns upon any of the above, this could produce feelings of shame. You may feel as though you have not lived up to expectations placed upon you by family members, society, or even your own (younger self) beliefs. This can be harmful. Getting to a place of feeling free from other people's opinions and judgment, and free even from your own as well, is an important step in releasing unnecessary shame.

Blame is to find fault with. Blame is the opposite of praise. When someone is morally responsible for doing something wrong, their actions are blameworthy. Often times we blame ourselves for our past experiences which were not our fault. If we can switch the blame from ourselves to the person or people that caused those experiences, then we can find space for releasing these emotions. For any of you reading out there, what happened to you when you were a child was not your fault. If another person in your life did something to you without your consent and you had no control over it and they hurt you to your core, they are fully responsible for those actions, not you. Those actions were not your fault. You did nothing wrong. This is very important to understand. Blaming ourselves leads to shame and guilt and these emotions have the power to cripple us. If we do not acknowledge these feelings and work with them, they continue to hold power over us. This is exactly the piece we need to heal. We take our power back when we release these emotions.

Guilt is that pervasive feeling that you have done something wrong or have caused harm in some way. Guilt can stem from a belief that you have failed in some way or have not met some expectation of yourself or others. Guilt is a natural emotion and can also be a positive experience to create change. But it is when guilt is pervasive or unwarranted that it can be damaging and unhealthy.

Through receiving unconditional support, such as through a therapist, professional material like ours, a trusted friend, support groups or other organizations, we can start to release and unveil the heaviness that we have been carrying around all of this. Unchecked emotions can cause us to seek some forms of escape and pleasure outside of ourselves. Sometimes, we do anything to avoid our emotions even though avoidance is detrimental. This is how shame, blame, and guilt can bind us. But we are now learning how to heal.

There are many more emotions that we experience throughout our lives. As we have mentioned, we aren't always tuned into our emotions. Sometimes we are in a very uncomfortable place, somewhere *in between* our emotions.

We are not yelling in anger, we are not crying in tears, we are not happy with laughter, and so on. We can be somewhere else. It can range from feeling uncomfortable to feeling awful, but our first response is to avoid these feelings because they can be overwhelming. We never quite stop long enough to **open a dialogue with our emotions.** We don't stop everything we are doing and deeply ask, "What is really going on here?" But times like these are a great opportunity to ask, because this is where the uncovering happens. We tried it for ourselves. We stopped. We asked. We waited for a reply. The reply might be "I just don't know," but it is still a reply. This can be a scary place for people. It can feel like an empty vortex or a darkness without answers. This can be a place containing confusion, frustration, possibly even fear. But this is where it can all begin. There is deep healing in uncovering your true emotions. This is where you begin to open your own unique dialogue.

Journal Entry from Ann

I met my abuser when I was about ten years old. This person befriended me in our neighborhood. I actually really liked this person and was grateful to have an adult male be part of my life. Although my father was present in the home, he wasn't present emotionally or in any other way available to me. I liked the attention that this older man, who was fifteen years older, gave to me. As I grew over the years, he did all the things a male mentor for a young person could do. He talked to me about things that were important, talked to me about friendships, came to my basketball and softball games, and allowed me to be part of his family. I loved this. Because I felt like I belonged, not something I felt in my own family of origin. The switch here happened when I was thirteen and the sexual abuse started.

I was completely confused about the situation. In my young thirteen-year-old mind, having known this person since I was ten, I felt I must trust that this was the way things were supposed to be. Having been told to keep it a secret, I did. Not having the maturity to understand the psychological damage that was being done, my thirteen-year-old self started to blame myself and believed that I had done something wrong. I wanted to keep this family part of my life so the abuse continued, and it wasn't till I was in therapy years later that I realized I had shifted blame on myself. This abuse went on for a period of time. I felt em-

barrassed and ashamed. I often wondered what could I have possibly done that would have caused this to happen?

That shame bound me for years. I kept that secret for a very, very long time, but it permeated every aspect of my life. It took hold of me and created so much disharmony in the core of who I was. This is called toxic shame.

Only through the loving support of my therapist was I able to see through this and start to heal it. This concept of Toxic Shame is not new. It's at the foundation of so much trauma. There are many books written about the subject. One in particular is called Healing the Shame That Binds You, *by John Bradshaw. Along with therapy I watched his videos and read his books. All of this helped me to heal. All of this helped me with my healing journey which still continues today. I use self-inquiry always to assess and address emotions, behaviors, and distractions that arise. Soul healing is a life journey while we are here. Be kind to yourself.*

. . . .

Pause For Curiosity

On the following pages you will find the six core emotions along with their related emotions in each category. Take some time to familiarize yourself with these emojis, words, and lists.

How many can you identify?

Which of the words in each category do you resonate with most often?

Which feelings have you intimately experienced yourself?

Are there any of these that you have *never* experienced?

What main emotion can you identify that you are working on in your life right now?

Some emotions are more easily identifiable than others. Asking these questions opens up an avenue of deeper healing, as we become more and more aware of the differences and nuances of this uncovering process.

. . . .

Uncover Your Emotions

Basic Emotions To Explore

Happy
The feeling of joy, love, or serenity, typically associated with peaceful, safe, and calm thoughts.

Sad

The emotional response to unhappiness, depression, or grief, often experienced by feelings of loneliness and melancholy.

Angry
A strong emotional state evidenced by annoyance, rage, or hatefulness, with an impulse to react to a perceived threat in an aggressive manner.

Fear

A response to a perceived danger, coinciding with a sense of worry, nervousness, or dread, in order to escape the source of fear.

Surprise

The reaction to unexpected circumstances involving wide eyes, raised eyebrows, along with feelings of being astonished, excited, or mind-blown. This can be a positive or negative experience.

Disgust

A visceral reaction to something offensive or loathsome, connected to feelings of outrage, disapproval, or repulsion.

Our lives change when we
figure out our real emotions.
We can stop avoiding,
hiding, and pretending now.
We empower ourselves when we ask:
"What is it that I am actually feeling?"

Happy

Peaceful
Joyful
Content
Calm
Loving
Safe
Grounded
Serene

Sad

Unhappy
Hopeless
Depressed
Discouraged
Lonely
Disappointed
Melancholy
Grief

Angry

Frustrated
Annoyed
Defensive
Critical
Rageful
Sarcastic
Hostile
Hateful

Fear

Anxious
Worried
Helpless
Nervous
Hyper-vigilant
Vulnerable
Fearful
Dread

Surprise

Shocked
Startled
Astonished
Mind-blown
Excited
Amazed
Baffled
Flabbergasted

Disgust

Sickened
Loathsome
Disillusioned
Outrage
Repulsed
WTF/Yuck Factor
Disapproval
Revulsion

Permission Slip

Please take the time now to fill out this slip for yourself.

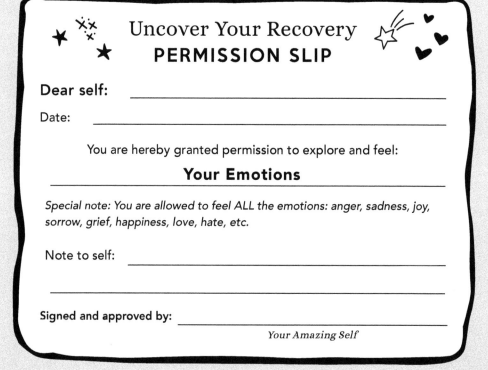

Uncover Your Recovery
PERMISSION SLIP

Dear self: _____

Date: _____

You are hereby granted permission to explore and feel:

Your Emotions
_____

Special note: You are allowed to feel ALL the emotions: anger, sadness, joy, sorrow, grief, happiness, love, hate, etc.

Note to self: _____

_____

Signed and approved by: _____

Your Amazing Self

Invitation/Challenge

Take advantage of this opportunity: Write something that you found meaningful or significant from this chapter.

Ann's List   BE KIND
to yourself

- [ ] Breathe
- [ ] Sleep, rest, take a nap
- [ ] Drink water
- [ ] Eat nourishing food
- [ ] Take a break from social media
- [ ] Shut off phone
- [ ] Ask for a hug
- [ ] Drink a cup of tea or coffee
- [ ] Watch a funny movie
- [ ] Laugh out loud
- [ ] Spend time in a garden
- [ ] Go to the library
- [ ] Stay in your pj's all day
- [ ] Take a bath or shower
- [ ] Purge old socks and underwear
- [ ] Go for a drive
- [ ] Get fresh air
- [ ] Go to the park
- [ ] Go to the beach
- [ ] Ask for support
- [ ] Go to the mountains
- [ ] Read a book

- [ ] Stretch
- [ ] Watch the sunrise or sunset
- [ ] Light a candle
- [ ] Give yourself a foot massage
- [ ] Have breakfast for dinner
- [ ] Compliment yourself
- [ ] Watch funny animal videos
- [ ] Take yourself out to eat
- [ ] Doodle, color, or draw
- [ ] Sing out loud
- [ ] Listen to birds
- [ ] Go for a bike ride
- [ ] Star gaze
- [ ] Buy a new pillow
- [ ] Buy yourself flowers
- [ ] Go for a walk
- [ ] Watch an old movie
- [ ] Go to a museum
- [ ] Go for a swim
- [ ] Pet a pet
- [ ] Practice gratitude
- [ ] Walk in the rain
- [ ] Get a massage or facial

MAURA'S MESSAGE FROM SPIRIT

The Fog told me a story today.

I am mysterious and soft,
thick with denseness, yet light as mist.
Rolling in unexpectedly,
An illusion of a barrier, blocking your sight.
Temporarily
A misty separation
Then . . . lifting and disappearing
Rolling back out
Just like magic
. . . just like you

You. You are the Fog.

CHAPTER 5

Uncover Your Behaviors

"Behavior is the mirror in which everyone shows their image."

- JOHANN WOLFGANG VON GOETHE

Many answers can be found by looking at our behaviors. We may be struggling to find our way, or just trying to feel better. When our lives are not going the way we plan, we may try anything to fix them. We may find ourselves exhausted, unhappy, or hurting. Our hearts are wounded. Our minds are crowded. Our lives may be filled with unfulfillment. We know this because we may have gone to extremes to find the answers. But sometimes those answers do not seem possible, and relief may not be in sight.

Is it even a reality to expect to escape pain and discomfort? Is it a reality to be able to make it all STOP? We may be experiencing racing thoughts, uneasy feelings, grief, sadness, even some madness and anger at times. We can't always recognize ourselves in the struggle. Yet we continue on when we feel like giving up. We might even feel an emptiness, or as if something is just missing. For example, Client A shared that throughout her experience of her child struggling with addiction she was consumed with racing thoughts of shame, blame, and doom. This brought her to ignore her own care in body, mind, and spirit. Without realizing it, she started shopping as a distraction for her pain. This behavior got out of control, and she ended up in debt. Which multiplied her feelings of shame and blame. Until she could identify this as a coping mechanism and an escape, she was not going to be able to change this unhealthy behavior pattern. When we have no awareness, we can't change things.

Have you struggled? Ask yourself if you use any of the following coping mechanisms such as alcohol, drugs, sex, or maybe food, gambling, or gaming? Perhaps binge-watching TV, like compulsively hitting "next episode" on Netflix. Maybe you are using unhealthy methods that you aren't even aware of. In our search for a way out of the pain, we reach for any number of things to distract or relieve ourselves from discomfort. Somewhere in the midst of our behaviors, there are things that seem acceptable and may even feel much like salvation. Many coping behaviors include spending, crafting, narcotics, cutting, therapy, smoking, pornography, exercising, using medications, nasal spray, gossip, drama, our phones, spiritual obsessions, food challenges, and more.

Perhaps your life is good. You have a house, food, money, and employment but there's this one thing that keeps persisting, that you can't seem to shake. You keep repeating a behavior that isn't healthy and you can't seem to stop. Take for instance shopping, like we mentioned above. You might realize that you are constantly on Amazon shopping for the latest thing. You know you are doing it; you realize it's not healthy, but then something comes up in your news feed while you are scrolling, and you just have to buy it. Add to cart. You buy it, there's excitement, then you feel bad about it or realize you didn't need it at all. Here's the deal though, we are inviting you to question and become aware of your own choices and behaviors. That is self-inquiry which you've already uncovered in a previous chapter. And as you are continuing to discover, this can bring us to the heart of the matter.

Patterns and behaviors didn't just start yesterday or the day before. More than likely, they started long ago. Repetitive patterns of behavior can be either healthy or unhealthy. It is the unhealthy patterns that we are addressing. These unhealthy patterns create the blocks and challenges in our everyday lives. Taking a closer look at these can bring us to the initial place of their creation. This awareness is one of the doorways to healing.

Client B shared that she is consistently disappointed that her girlfriend doesn't express her love through words. She feels that hearing the words "I love you" is so important in a relationship. She is sick and tired of always asking her girlfriend to say it. She feels if she has to ask it loses its value. On the other side of this her girlfriend expresses her love through gifts and spending quality time together. There's a lot of curiosity in this client's case. Client B came from a home where her father did not have the capacity to express his feelings in words, which is something she desperately needed and still does. Her girlfriend came from a home where it was not safe to express feelings in words.

In the behaviors above we identified their origin. The next steps after identifying are communication and healing in order for both partners in this relationship to get their needs met.

We can ask ourselves, how long have I been repeating certain behaviors? Continually picking the wrong partner, changing jobs, blaming ourselves for everything that's wrong, being overly responsible, continually people pleasing, enabling others, etc. Looking back, is there an age or specific incidents that you can remember where these behaviors or patterns began? The reason we are asking you to invest time in identifying behaviors is because this is a huge piece to your overall healing. This may take some time to explore. You may not even be aware yet of the power that unhealthy patterns have in your life.

. . . .

Here are some scenarios to consider for your own self-inquiry.

Were your parents super controlling?

Did they need to know where you were at all times?

Was there a coach or teacher that was condescending or unkind?

Did your religious education make you feel inadequate or oppressed?

Did your schoolwork reflect on your self-esteem or confidence?

Did you feel accepted in your friendship connections, or did you feel like the odd one out?

Have you always felt the need to measure up to others, in school, on a team or at work, etc.?

. . . .

After identifying and possibly seeing a connection to old stories and patterns, ask yourself what the similarities might be, in how you acted then and how you act today. Once we identify these patterns, we can change them. For instance, let's use the example of having controlling parents. This can show up in a multitude of ways later in life. You might become super rigid, only seeing black or white, and no gray. Or on the other hand you can give your power away and allow yourself to be controlled by someone else. This is mirroring the environment you grew up in. Identifying this gives you the opportunity to choose something different. Learning to compromise when you have been rigid, having healthy boundaries instead of being a doormat, and finding your own voice when you've never been heard, are all examples of changed behavior. When put into action and we investigate these behaviors, we disrupt the old patterns and create more permanent and lasting change. These questions can be explored verbally, or by using a journal, by sharing with a trusted friend or working through this alone. We believe in you. While this specific process of identifying behaviors can feel overwhelming and uncomfortable, we know from our own personal experiences that it works. Even small changes create enormous healing results.

Four steps to become more curious and aware of our behavior patterns:

1. Identify Behavior that you want to change.
2. Be honest about the extent of your behavior. You only need to know *what* the behavior is you would like to change. You do not need to know the why right now.
3. Choose an action. An action you commit to and repeat is one of the absolute fastest ways to change an unwanted behavior pattern.
4. Share it. Text it, post it, phone a friend, journal about it, talk to a therapist, etc. It doesn't need to make sense to anyone else but you.

Using the steps above, here are two examples you can consider.

Example 1: Maybe there is drama or chaos in your life.

1. A behavior you can identify that you want to change regarding this: Participating in gossip, complaining, repeating the story unnecessarily.

2. Be honest. Are you the one that's keeping the drama alive or making it worse by engaging constantly about the subject? How much is occupying your time, your day, your mind, and conversation?

3. What action are you committing to, in order to change this? Being aware is a first action. Then limiting your engagement. Before your next text or conversation, can you stop and shift your attention to something else? This is where the change happens. **This IS the shift**.

4. Share it. In this scenario, it can be sharing something positive, new, and different. You can talk about something else such as your hobbies, personal interests, current events in your own life. You can discuss accomplishments at work, or about your family, or your children, etc. Shifting the focus away from the unhealthy repetition of gossip to healthier choices is an extremely empowering victory.

Example 2: Family member has an addiction.

1. Identify a behavior you want to change regarding a family member having an addiction. Decide to no longer allow your own focus to be their lives, their choices, and their actions.

2. Be honest. Are you adding any value to the situation by complaining about it and trying to constantly fix or control it?

3. What action are you committing to in order to change this behavior? Being aware is the first step. Is there an outside source of support for yourself to help you? The only behavior we can change is our own so you can shift the attention back to your own behavior.

4. Share it. In this scenario, sharing your commitment to change your behavior can give others permission to change their own.

♡ Journal Entry from Ann

How we cope: What is a medicator? What is a pattern?

During your trip here on the planet with all its twists and turns, your mind, which likes to always be in charge, started finding ways to soothe itself, to soften the blows of disappointment, to soften the sadness. Your mind is a powerful thing, and it is especially good at telling our body stories. When we don't have proper tools in place though, we start coping with other things to help us to feel better. We call these things medicators, compulsions, addictions, self-soothing techniques. What they really are though are distractions that make you stop feeling the feelings.

When you have grown up in a home where there is zero permission to feel any other way than happy, your body shuts down the other emotions. If you were told to never be angry you have no way to identify it. It can create a freeze response in your body, mind, and spirit.

The medicators work like this. Your mother yells at you, you try to explain, you get shut down. You are mad, with no outlet. You head to the fridge, there is cake. Cake is something you get when you are good. You eat the cake because you think it will make you feel better. You have now stuffed your anger down inside you along with cake, but you have not addressed your emotions, you stuffed them instead. It's not healthy as you now know to stuff your anger or eat your anger.

Another scenario. You are in an abusive home where your dad yells all the time and screams at you, there is never a quiet conversation, everything is yelling. You become a screamer in your own life, all the time, no one likes this about you, they call you bitchy or bossy. You feel alone. You decide to have a drink to feel better. It takes the edge off of you. No more being bitchy for now.

The scenarios are endless of what our minds will convince us to do under the misguided attempt to help us feel better. It can cajole us at every opportunity. Here's the thing though, with no awareness of healthy coping skills we will go to the manufactured ones that society perpetuates, things that are outside of us. We will eat food, we will drink alcohol, we will shop, we will join the gym (and go seven days a week), we will work to excess because our work-family loves us. We will gamble, because the rush of winning feels good for a moment. We will have sex with random people because it helps us forget for a moment. We will play video games, scroll incessantly on social media, we will talk non-stop without a breath and never ever, will we stop. You get the idea. These are all distractions to get us outside the truth of what's really happening.

It's one thing to have a piece of cake when you are feeling down, it's another thing altogether to eat unhealthy food every single day. It's one thing to have a drink when you socialize, it's a whole other ballgame when we drink every day to cope. When these patterns of unhealthy behavior set in, they are nothing more than our mind directing our body to cope with the inner feelings that we have never been able to identify or express. It's also important to note that medicators are not always negative, they can keep us safe and alive while we are working on ourselves. As we become more curious and aware we can alter and change our choices and behaviors that we use as medicators. Be gentle and kind to yourself.

Take a moment and go back to the bags you've been carrying, as discussed in Chapter 2. Let's take some burden off thinking that all these medicators and patterns are solely your fault. During your curiosity, as we also covered in Chapter 2, if you peeked inside your bags and realized that your dad had a drink every night when he came home from work and that your mom was always at the mall the day after she got paid, this became the setup for you. You learned these behaviors, patterns, and coping skills at home. However, as adults now we do need to take personal responsibility for the choices that dictate our behaviors that we can now identify.

Once we become aware of what influences us, we can change our behaviors. For example, even the media with all its advertisements of happy people drinking, shopping, getting their hair done, and enjoying fancy cars, vacations, etc. are selling you the idea that "if you buy it, you will feel better." The advertising industry is genius in how it manipulates us. They spend millions of dollars creating campaigns to suck us into their false advertising. The narrative is that we "are not enough as is." This is what creates a sense of low self-esteem. Self-esteem and self-worth are strongly intertwined. A low sense of self can be compounded by a lot of the traumas and past experiences that have happened throughout our lives. Our low self-esteem can then create a void within us that advertisers are trying to fill. They are selling us on the idea of our own perceived lack. When we believe something is missing, instead of looking within ourselves, we've learned to look outside of ourselves to fill this inside void.

Similarly, social media use and abuse is more rampant than ever and can directly connect to our feelings of worth and self-esteem. How many likes do you get on Facebook, Instagram, TikTok, etc. How many times do you see your friends, or others, and think their lives are great and yours sucks? How many pictures, sayings, and others' experiences lead us to believe we are always missing out on something in our own lives? Don't get us started on how these social media giants use artificial intelligence to suck us in even further. We are a product to them and thus we are sellable. Our media feeds will contain everything we talk about and search for. It can be unnerving to know that technology can be so extremely invasive, even though it is also an invaluable tool. It is important to maintain a healthy balance, to be mindful of how we use social media, and how our lives are affected by it. It is okay to give yourself permission to review your daily usage and make changes as needed.

As we can see, choosing our behaviors affect all areas of our lives. We cannot change behavior patterns by "thinking" about them. Taking personal responsibility and physical action steps are what is needed to create lasting, successful change.

Permission Slip

Please take the time now to fill out this slip for yourself.

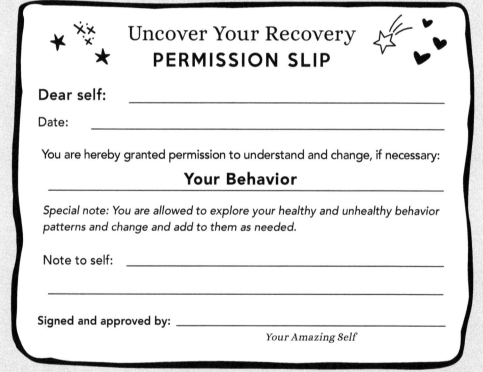

Uncover Your Recovery
PERMISSION SLIP

Dear self: _____

Date: _____

You are hereby granted permission to understand and change, if necessary:

Your Behavior
_____

Special note: You are allowed to explore your healthy and unhealthy behavior patterns and change and add to them as needed.

Note to self: _____

_____

Signed and approved by: _____

Your Amazing Self

Invitation/Challenge

Take advantage of this opportunity: Write something that you found meaningful or significant from this chapter.

Ann's List

BE KIND
to yourself

- [ ] Breathe
- [ ] Sleep, rest, take a nap
- [ ] Drink water
- [ ] Eat nourishing food
- [ ] Take a break from social media
- [ ] Shut off phone
- [ ] Ask for a hug
- [ ] Drink a cup of tea or coffee
- [ ] Watch a funny movie
- [ ] Laugh out loud
- [ ] Spend time in a garden
- [ ] Go to the library
- [ ] Stay in your pj's all day
- [ ] Take a bath or shower
- [ ] Purge old socks and underwear
- [ ] Go for a drive
- [ ] Get fresh air
- [ ] Go to the park
- [ ] Go to the beach
- [ ] Ask for support
- [ ] Go to the mountains
- [ ] Read a book

- [ ] Stretch
- [ ] Watch the sunrise or sunset
- [ ] Light a candle
- [ ] Give yourself a foot massage
- [ ] Have breakfast for dinner
- [ ] Compliment yourself
- [ ] Watch funny animal videos
- [ ] Take yourself out to eat
- [ ] Doodle, color, or draw
- [ ] Sing out loud
- [ ] Listen to birds
- [ ] Go for a bike ride
- [ ] Star gaze
- [ ] Buy a new pillow
- [ ] Buy yourself flowers
- [ ] Go for a walk
- [ ] Watch an old movie
- [ ] Go to a museum
- [ ] Go for a swim
- [ ] Pet a pet
- [ ] Practice gratitude
- [ ] Walk in the rain
- [ ] Get a massage or facial

MAURA'S MESSAGE FROM SPIRIT

The Rain told me a story today.

As the Rain told me a story
The thunder and lightning jumped in.
Deep crackling, rolling sounds,
The quickest sword-strikes of vibrant light.
The cleansing, cold, down pour of a fluid power.
Unpredictable. Beautiful.
Without explanation.
Renewing the freshness.
True to their splendid nature.
You are Thunder and Lightning.

You. You are the Rain.

CHAPTER 6

Uncover and Discover Your Higher Power

"May you recognize in your life the presence, power, and light of your soul. May you realize that you are never alone, that your soul in its brightness and belonging connects you intimately with the rhythm of the universe. May you have respect for your own individuality and difference."

- JOHN O'DONOHUE

A Higher Power is considered a power or energy greater than our human selves. The world uses multiple terms, different titles, and many concepts to describe God. Maybe your beliefs have grown or changed over the years. Maybe your concepts are no longer the same as they were in your family of origin. As we have mentioned, we grew up in the Roman Catholic Church, believing in God, Jesus, the Saints, Angels, and the Holy Spirit. These were the terms we were familiar with. What terms were you familiar with growing up? We have since changed and expanded our beliefs. Have you?

This is a great opportunity to explore the concepts regarding your beliefs and faith.

When we get curious and ask ourselves to examine what we believe in today, we can begin to become more comfortable with terms, words, and descriptions that are in alignment with who we are now. You can ask yourself what feels right for you, what resonates. **For You**. If you did not have the limits of your family, your friends, or society, what would you start saying to describe your own personal relationship with Spirit? Maybe you find yourself presently having no faith at all. That's perfectly understandable with all the challenges facing us today. It may be difficult to discern what or who to believe in. This is an invitation to examine and be curious right now. Can you connect to anything? For example, maybe you can appreciate the amazing beauty and diversity of nature, the cycles and seasons, the ebbs and flows of the power of the natural world. Each day we have a new opportunity to open up and explore.

The following is an excerpt, from Al-Anon:

> *"While walking through the woods one day, I was surprised to hear a child's voice. I followed the sound, trying in vain to understand the child's words. When I spotted a boy perched on a rock, I realized why his words had made no sense; he was repeating the alphabet. 'Why are you saying your ABCs so many times?' I asked him. The child replied, 'I'm saying my prayers.' I couldn't help but laugh. 'Prayers? All I hear is the alphabet.' Patiently the child explained, 'Well, I don't know all the words, so I give God the letters. God knows what I'm trying to say.' The story is a reminder that prayer is for the person praying, not for God, who knows what we are going through without explanation. With prayer we are willing to be helped. The meaning behind prayers comes from our heart, not from our words. Prayer is a personal form of communication. You can pray by consciously thinking, writing, creating, feeling, and hoping. Whether we reach deep inside ourselves or turn outward toward the majesty of nature, it is the spirit of prayer rather than its form that matters."*
>
> - Anonymous

We love this story about prayer because it encompasses an expansive viewpoint, as prayer is not a one-size-fits-all container.

Our parents, grandparents, and ancestors didn't have the freedom to openly question their religious beliefs like we have the freedom to do today.

It still may be hard to consider going against the belief systems of your family of origin, but this is crucial to your own personal development and deep healing. Remember we are getting curious and questioning everything.

We invite you to get curious about what spiritually resonates for you right now at this point in your life. It might take some time. Know that your beliefs and terms may change as your own true connection develops and unfolds. AND THAT IS OKAY! YOU HAVE PERMISSION. Little by little, you will start to learn what feels right for you. Do not be afraid. This is the time to be kind to yourself, release judgment and be open to exploration. Your connection and comfort will grow stronger as you develop your own intimate relationship with Spirit.

This is also an opportunity to practice saying some new terms. It's like trying them on to see what fits in your own vocabulary and determining what feels right. Again, it might take a little time. It may be new for you. This is why it's a good idea to surround yourself with people you resonate with; those who will not judge or criticize. This is a process. You can also honor it by not judging yourself. In a short amount of time, a shift happens, and you will actually feel empowered. We believe that this is one of the challenges of religion today. There is a lot of hypocrisy. When it comes to religion there seems to be so much confusion in the world. Every generation has questions. Some question the dogmatic and rigid principles of the religion of our ancestry. It is not about who is right and who is wrong. Judgment takes away from the real messages of love and light and divinity.

Speaking of Divinity, we personally use the following terms, including terms to describe Mother Nature and Mother Earth as a Living, Breathing, Divine Being:

Highest Light of Divinity	Great Spirit of the Earth
Universal Love	Mother Nature
Divine Light	Gaia
The Universe	Mother Earth
Angels of God	God
White Light	Divine Forces of Nature
The God of Your	The Divine Mother in all
Understanding	Her Holy Names

Using your curiosity and awareness tools, experiment. See what feels right for your own connection to a Higher Power or energy. It is our experience that a Power greater than ourselves can change our lives. We invite you to uncover and discover what that power or energy is for you.

These concepts might be bringing up some discomfort and fears. It is challenging to release ourselves from our old perceptions and beliefs. But doing this has so many benefits and we don't have to do this work on our own. Clarifying our spiritual connection can help us feel supported, safe, and grounded. It can help us heal. It gives us the opportunity to know what a personal experience with Spirit feels like.

There are many ways we can call and connect to this power. Such as prayer, meditation, ritual, organized services, mass, and spiritual groups. We can use journaling, angel cards, creating altars, spending more time in nature, reading materials, and inspirational music. **Give yourself permission** to develop your own spirituality and connection from the place of who you are today. As we have mentioned, this can change over time and continue to develop.

If you don't know where to start, you can start with hope. Spirituality can offer us a light in the darkness. And that's where hope comes in.

Hope (Oxford Publishing definition)

A feeling of expectation and desire for a certain thing to happen.

A feeling of trust.

Hope is finding confidence in something other than ourselves. It gives us a sense of possibilities. It leads us away from the feelings of hopelessness and helplessness. Sometimes, hope is all we have. It can be a basis and foundation for us to build on. And we can begin to build our spirituality upon this. Sometimes holding onto hope can be what gets us through the most difficult of times. We can believe in something good, even when we don't yet see it happening, much like nature. Hope is a lifeline, a place we can find some peace. It creates a feeling that not all is lost or impossible. Hope is a bridge that can lead us from despair to possibilities, optimism, and joy. Just like nature has cycles of life and death, growth and loss and rebirth, hope can support us and guide us to a belief in something greater than ourselves. This can birth our own spirituality.

Another element of cultivating our spirituality is the concept of forgiveness. In our experiences, we have found hope and forgiveness to be two key components that have supported us in our healing journey. As part of your recovery, the concept of forgiveness will most likely arise. It's not an easy subject to discuss. Such a rabbit hole we could go down in why we "should" forgive and why we "should" forget.

Forgiveness (Merriam's definition)

to cease to feel resentment against (an offender): pardon forgive one's enemies

Forget (Merriam's definition)

to lose the remembrance of: be unable to think of or recall

Ann: I recently said out loud, "There would be no such thing as forgiveness if religion wasn't a thing." While I'm not sure that's entirely true, it's something to be curious about for sure. As already stated, I was raised Roman Catholic. We love to talk all about forgiveness. How important it is as humans to ask the God of our understanding to forgive our trespasses and for us to forgive those who trespass against us. It's indoctrinated into our being as born Christians. I cannot speak for other religions; they are not my lived experience.

What I can speak to is the need for curiosity about what forgiveness really means to us. I believe that it cannot be forced, coerced, or something we are made to do. It needs to be lived into action. Meaning if I choose to forgive another for their wrongdoing against me, that's my choice to make, when, how, where and in what manner. In recovering our healing, we are seeking to heal, in most instances, the traumas that were put upon us without our consent.

Forgiving this takes time, like mourning grief, there is no clock, it is a unique process for each person.

Forgetting is a whole other matter. We've heard this phrase often. "You should forgive and forget." Seriously, that parroting of handed down words from one generation to the next doesn't work anymore. We are living in such a time that we get to make our own choices about our body, mind, and spirit.

What did I do regarding my abuse and forgiveness? I chose to empower myself with healing. The idea of forgiveness was never about absolving the other person for me. It was about freeing my body, mind, and spirit from the unhealthy attachment to the situation that permeated my entire being for many years. That was freedom. I have not forgotten, I never will. It took so much patience, kindness toward myself, unconditional support, and a desire to be free without fear.

Your friends, therapist, or support people might offer this approach to you. They might say it's time to forgive the other person. I say nope. I say you decide what that will look like for you. You decide if keeping the situation alive inside your essence is worth it, or if releasing the ties to it feels better. Be patient. If someone or multiple people have hurt you, your healing comes first. Letting them off the hook comes way last, if ever. This is where religion can get in the way of our deeper healing. The constructs of many religious beliefs that are steeped in control have a vast hold on our lives through our ancestral, generational roots. We are allowed to be curious, to be more aware, to rethink, and to change our thoughts as we need for our ultimate healing and peace.

. . . .

Questions to Think About

What are your thoughts about forgiveness?

What are your thoughts about forgetting?

Give yourself some space to be curious about what these two ideas mean on your healing journey.

Can you look at forgiveness as an act of compassion for yourself?

Can you give yourself permission to release the emotions and feelings about a situation, so you have more peace?

. . . .

It's not an easy step, but the rewards can be amazing. Turning forgiveness around becomes a gift you give yourself for the hurtful treatment you received, and it can be life-changing. Forgetting can be turned around also, becoming a reminder to yourself of the bravery and courage you have within you. Being brave and courageous in times of crimes of betrayal against you is worthy of noticing. Along with being brave and courageous, you are also resilient. Resilience means that you can never go back to the you that you were before your hurts, but that you can move into the newer version of yourself, wiser and more empowered. If you are reading this book, no matter where you are in your healing process, you are brave, courageous, and resilient.

♡ Journal Entry from Ann

As far back as I can remember I had been searching for religion to offer me something that I could relate to. In my younger years I went to church because I had to or else I would be grounded. Moving through my life though I knew I loved Jesus, but not in the way I felt like I was supposed to. It was more duty than it was relationship, it was what religion wanted me to do, not feel. After the shame of my first divorce, I felt even more removed from religion and God. In the eyes of the church I was a sinner, but I still received communion even though I wasn't supposed to. Religion still felt like something I needed to get, but it continued to remain out of reach. My second marriage gave me more insight about religion. I was older and had been practicing yoga and being more curious about so many alternative ideas and philosophies. I still felt like I was getting religion wrong and started trying out so many churches. I landed again in the Catholic church because it felt comfortable and familiar, but the feeling was still the same. I went through the motions but didn't follow the rules that are set out by that religion, so the shame was always following me.

With my second divorce and again, more lived experience of being older, I started to be even more curious about spirituality instead of the idea of religion. Spirituality was being talked about more in the world, the people I knew were challenging their own religious upbringing and I started to feel less shame. I was free to explore this feeling I always had about Jesus in a different way. I started reading more books and listening to inspirational things that offered an alternative thought on religion. I bought A Course In Miracles, *by Marianne Williamson. I read the* Bhagavad Gita *from the yoga tradition and* Beyond Belief *by Elaine Pagels. I was curious all the time.*

Then around 2007, I found angel cards, oracle cards, and inspirational card decks. This is where my connection to Spirit became so expansive and so open that it led me to here in the now of now, writing this book. If you have been struggling with your religious upbringing and have been feeling confused about where to start or how to begin here is what I did that might be helpful:

1. *Find a deck of oracle, inspirational, angel or healing cards in a bookstore or online that resonates.*
2. *Each day pick a card or a few cards and read the messages. Sit with the cards and messages and be curious.*
3. *Use a journal to write down your feelings about how the card resonates in your life. If you don't want to write it down, take a picture with your phone, look at it during the day.*
4. *Start to watch the patterns that show up and be curious about how the cards you pick seem to be possibly in sync with what you are going through or what your inner self has been saying to you.*
5. *Try doing this for longer than thirty days, it takes a while for the consistency and synchronicity to start to build more awareness inside of you.*

It's not foolproof, but for me it made me feel like something bigger than me was at work in my life, that each card I pulled resonated for me on a particular day. I was able to see that there was a pattern of picking the same card sometimes, and I felt supported by an unknown something. It made me more curious and strengthened my belief that something far greater than myself was working with me for my highest good. It helped me build connection to the elusive God of my understanding, to the Jesus of my childhood, because I finally felt supported by something I couldn't really explain to anyone but could feel in myself. I still pull cards, I journal most days, I do something quiet for myself each morning because morning is my time. This practice resonated for me, and I can say that the idea of religion, with its duty and rules that made me feel bad about myself is behind me, and my heart is truly open to a Spirit greater than I can ever imagine.

Permission Slip

Please take the time now to fill out this slip for yourself.

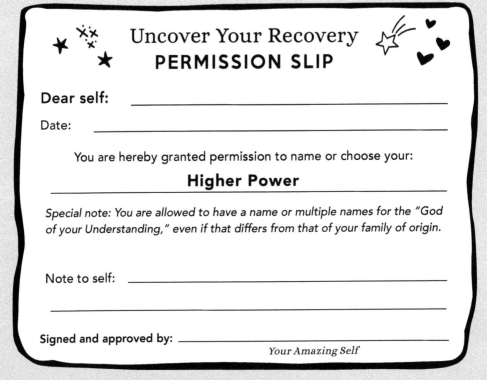

Uncover Your Recovery
PERMISSION SLIP

Dear self: _____

Date: _____

You are hereby granted permission to name or choose your:

Higher Power

_____

Special note: You are allowed to have a name or multiple names for the "God of your Understanding," even if that differs from that of your family of origin.

Note to self: _____

_____

Signed and approved by: _____

Your Amazing Self

Invitation/Challenge

Take advantage of this opportunity: Write something that you found meaningful or significant from this chapter.

Ann's List
BE KIND
to yourself

- [ ] Breathe
- [ ] Sleep, rest, take a nap
- [ ] Drink water
- [ ] Eat nourishing food
- [ ] Take a break from social media
- [ ] Shut off phone
- [ ] Ask for a hug
- [ ] Drink a cup of tea or coffee
- [ ] Watch a funny movie
- [ ] Laugh out loud
- [ ] Spend time in a garden
- [ ] Go to the library
- [ ] Stay in your pj's all day
- [ ] Take a bath or shower
- [ ] Purge old socks and underwear
- [ ] Go for a drive
- [ ] Get fresh air
- [ ] Go to the park
- [ ] Go to the beach
- [ ] Ask for support
- [ ] Go to the mountains
- [ ] Read a book

- [ ] Stretch
- [ ] Watch the sunrise or sunset
- [ ] Light a candle
- [ ] Give yourself a foot massage
- [ ] Have breakfast for dinner
- [ ] Compliment yourself
- [ ] Watch funny animal videos
- [ ] Take yourself out to eat
- [ ] Doodle, color, or draw
- [ ] Sing out loud
- [ ] Listen to birds
- [ ] Go for a bike ride
- [ ] Star gaze
- [ ] Buy a new pillow
- [ ] Buy yourself flowers
- [ ] Go for a walk
- [ ] Watch an old movie
- [ ] Go to a museum
- [ ] Go for a swim
- [ ] Pet a pet
- [ ] Practice gratitude
- [ ] Walk in the rain
- [ ] Get a massage or facial

MAURA'S MESSAGE FROM SPIRIT

Rock told me a story today.

Oh solid Rock of the Earth.
Broken into pieces for your collecting and building.
Long since have we received any appreciation
for our wondrous stability and power.
Taken for granted and neglected.
Our many shapes, sizes, and colors.
The strength of our solid, supporting nature,
chipped away, yet holding strong.
You have forgotten.

You. You are a Rock.

CHAPTER 7

Pulling Together Body, Mind, and Spirit

"Live from the inside out. Your mind, body, and spirit are interconnected. Nourish your soul with mental and physical wellness."

- JANET TAYLOR SPENCE

Body, mind, and spirit are the main components of our individual uniqueness. Understanding each of these separately is not enough, we need to understand that they work together to create flow, balance, and harmony. It is about fluidity. Body, mind, and spirit are powerful, living, breathing forces that are constantly present in our lives, whether we are aware of them or not. We need to be curious and keep an open mind when diving into these concepts. Looking at philosophies and beliefs from all different cultures and systems we can be better informed and educated about what resonates with our unique selves. In some cultures, the approach to healing encompasses the whole person; body, mind, and spirit, yet in other cultures, the approach looks at symptoms and organ systems separately. An example would be feeling run down and tired and going to the doctor.

In this scenario, this doctor might want to only deal with your physical symptoms and possibly prescribe medicine. This limits the ability to check in with our own body, mind, and spirit in its totality. We may trust this doctor because we have been taught that they know more. We have not been encouraged or taught to tap into our innate, intuitive wisdom about what we feel might be wrong. Using the same scenario, an alternative or functional medicine doctor might ask questions about our whole self, current or past circumstances, including emotional challenges as well as physical, and give us an opportunity to offer our thoughts. This is a whole system approach.

When we are not connected to all three aspects of body, mind, and spirit, that's when it seems the doctor, the teacher, the lawyer, the coach, appear to know better or know more than we do. All the "important" people with initials after their name know more about your body, your mind, your spirit than you do, right? Not so much. We have been lulled into this place of false narrative for so long and it's time to wake up. Blending all medical, spiritual, and psychological philosophies can have a more positive affect on our overall healing. Collaboration and mutual respect are key. We are fortunate to live in such times that we can explore and educate ourselves.

Here is an example of a whole system approach. You need surgery. After surgery, the doctor and care team ensure that you have emotional support for the physical and emotional trauma that takes place during any surgery. This whole system approach ensures that you have access to additional options such as holistic practices, spiritual support, alternative modalities such as Reiki, Healing Touch, massage, *as well as* prescription medications, physical therapy, checkups, and other medicinal options. This is starting to happen in lots of places in the world and when we all become more educated and aware, we help ourselves and others.

As humans we have separated ourselves. In our recovery, we need to connect to the sacred place within ourselves that completes the triangle of body, mind, and spirit. When we all work together, regardless of professional titles that separate us sometimes, we empower and create mutual respect for the higher good of all.

One of the most significant and effective things we can do is get curious about the forces of body, mind, and spirit in our own individual lives. No one else can experience this for you, except yourself. It is an exploration, it is uncovering an exciting adventure, full of wonder and awe. You can be led and walked through processes, but the deep uncovering comes from you. You can do it. Chances are high that if you have gotten this far on the journey then you are ready to uncover even more treasures filled with even deeper gifts.

Body

The miracle we sometimes take for granted. The structure of ourselves that needs food, air, and water, that deals with physical conditions and illnesses. The vehicle we use for exercising, hugging, speaking, hearing, seeing, smelling, touching. We do all this with the physical body, and yet, do we ever really study the body? The many systems of the body? The way those systems work together to keep us running? We would be amazed at the miracle they truly are. If only we had a deeper interest and understanding of our anatomy and physiology, it would open a whole world of wonder. Yet few of us ever do really live with the highest respect for such a magnificent, unique vehicle. The systems of the body are bombarded each day with overstimulation, environmental conditions, extreme stressors, multiple influences both negative and positive, an assault on all our senses, and an overwhelming amount of things to process. Our body, this one body we are given, needs to sustain us for the length of our lives here on this planet. We can't think ourselves into wellness with our minds nor can we pray it into health through Spirit without honoring our physical selves. They all work together. And because they all work together, we need to question everything.

Sometimes, we need to use our voices that have been stifled to identify our emotions. We need to connect with the sensations that arise in our bodies, become aware of their location, and allow ourselves to feel them in order to process them.

Recovery means we need to reclaim ourselves for ourselves.

As we've stated, we need to actively participate in our healing and not just go for the quick fix or wait for someone else to heal us. The world of somatic (body centered) healing is wide open now giving us permission to feel and explore. Going beyond talk therapy, somatic approach to healing is finally mainstream. We need to research, we need to ask questions, we need to learn to tap into our inner, limitless resources of wisdom. This is our birthright and gift from the Divine to connect to our amazing physical existence.

If you are intimidated by any body movement options, use your curiosity and explore. There are many free practices on the internet. Curiosity and research allow you to find something that resonates with you.

Mind

The place of our thoughts. The place we process information, ideas, knowledge and mental acuity. The place of our to-do lists, our planning, our reminiscing. One of the places where we store our memories, our beliefs, and the place that houses our words and our images. Some believe we can THINK our way through anything, that clear intentions will change our lives and that our thoughts have all the power. And yes, the mind is one of the strongest powers we possess. Our thoughts are responsible for so much that happens in our lives but even though our thoughts are powerful, they certainly do not work alone. The mind is a powerful place, but it is even more powerful when we realize the connection the mind has to both the body and spirit. Tapping into this power and using it in conjunction with the other components gives us an accelerated opportunity to grow, heal, and change.

Spirit

That deep heart space within us. The one center that can connect us all on a spiritual level. We all have intuition; we all have a wise teacher that resides within us. We have an opportunity to tune in and ask what is guiding us. Is it the voice of the ego or the voice of Spirit? Is it our mind or is it in the deeper place of our knowing? Even though the voice of ego holds benefits, it can also be extremely judgmental. The voice of Spirit is unconditional, accepting, and loving. It can be difficult to discern the ego mind from Spirit. This is why we teach the importance of being still and quiet, listening to the voice of sacredness, instead of our racing minds. We can invite the mind to drop its awareness into the physical body to hear and connect to the sacred voice of Spirit.

It doesn't get much more powerful than that.

Spiritual Bypassing

It's important to note this concept. Psychotherapist, John Welwood, coined the term "spiritual bypassing" and it is an important topic. Spiritual bypassing is when we attempt to heal our wounds, without actually doing the healing WORK itself. It can be a dangerous habit to form, as it is a way to avoid including the body, mind, and emotions that are necessary for productive healing. Bypassing occurs when we find ourselves using spiritual concepts, affirmations, and just going through the motions without actually experiencing the hands-on process of facing deep, unresolved issues. It may also involve working with someone we view as an "expert" or leader in a certain healing field. Nobody has better answers and direction for your life than you do, yet we give our power away to perceived gurus, higher ups, etc.

We can be misguided into believing that if we use external actions alone, like praying harder, meditating, using affirmations, and toxic positivity, that we can reach the state of healing we are looking for. These can all be a support, but they cannot be a replacement for addressing suppressed traumas. Suppressed traumas need to be processed. Since the foundation of spiritual bypassing is avoidance; pretending that everything is okay when it's not will catch up to most of us.

It is priceless to finally realize that allowing ourselves to go through the uncomfortable process of feeling our full range of emotions can set us free.

Ask yourself the following questions with the intention of truly listening to the answers without judgment. This is a great time to grab a journal or some paper and write down your answers.

What does my Body need?

Food, water, movement, sex?

Is it detox, chanting, healthy touch, massage, hugs?

Is it hair care, hand cream, new clothes, socks, underwear, a hair tie?

Or something else? Add your own.

What does my Mind need?

Reading, enhanced learning, puzzles, mind challenges, engaging conversation?

Is it mantras, reviewing inner thoughts and running commentary of mind chatter, worry, changing outdated beliefs?

Or something else? Add your own.

What does my Spirit need?

Connection, community, prayer, nature, healing, quiet time, love, peace, gratitude, hope?

Is it affirmations, Spiritual assistance, resources?

Is it values, purpose, awareness, Source/God connection?

Or something else? Add your own.

. . . .

Personal Story from Maura

The body is something I happen to know a lot about. You see, I've been abusing mine for years. Mostly with food, trauma, and neglect. Like most of us, we have heard repeatedly that we need to "eat right and exercise." Believe it or not, this is useless information. Words are powerful. "Eat right." Already this indicates you are doing something wrong. "Exercise." I don't know about you, but I grew up with nuns, teachers, and coaches that used exercise as punishment. That did not set up a healthy relationship with that suggestion. Neither of these two pieces of advice were ever going to help me. How about you?

These days my relationship to food and body movement has changed drastically. This has come at the expensive price of fifty years' worth of struggle and pain. My food issues and body image challenges started at a very young age, mixed with being sexually molested before the age of eight years old until I was twelve, all created a ton of dysfunction for me.

It has taken me decades to unravel the connection of healthy food and body movement, and to discover respect and love for my physical self. All of which is an ongoing process.

This layer can get very complicated when you add emotions, thoughts, and in-grained beliefs, which all tie back into the body, mind, and spirit connection.

When you have thoughts of shame, guilt, and embarrassment, when you are hiding and suppressing secrets, and when you are confused, the confusion invades how you feel about yourself, your body, and your thoughts all around what is happening. When you are too young to understand all the pieces and what is really going on, you can short circuit a healthy bond and relationship with your young, developing self. It affects everything, your body, your mind, and your spirit.

At a young age, you do not have the tools or capability of processing all of this, so trauma occurs. This trauma is beyond physiological. All three levels of body, mind, and spirit are wounded, altered, affected.

What we are learning now is that we need to **engage** the body, mind, and spirit in order to allow proper amounts of energy, vibration, and healing to flow. Otherwise, we create interruptions that have serious ramifications on our peace of mind and our complete health.

This is where we can begin to heal.

When I was nine, as I have mentioned, I was put on a diet, brought to Weight Watchers, and embarrassed and humiliated, even though that was not my mother's intention. She wanted me to develop healthy knowledge and awareness about weight and food. Instead, what I acquired was shame and guilt. All three of my siblings were slim. When chocolate pudding was made for everyone else, Jell-O was made for me. When they were eating one thing, eyes were on me for what was okay and not okay for me to eat. There were "their snacks" and "my snacks." Their celery and my celery. Their celery had cream cheese on it. I love celery. I *loved celery and cream cheese. But I wasn't allowed to have it.*

It wasn't until recently that I put all this together. I cannot tell you how many times I've bought celery only to watch it rot in my frig, to be (almost happily) thrown away.

So, this is my apology.

Dear Celery, I'm Sorry

Celery with cream cheese, but not for you
Yours is as plain as can be.
No matter what it is that I seem to do
It's like they just can't see

I'm being punished because I'm so big
But I keep getting bigger to be seen
I don't understand what's going on
Or why they're being so mean

I can't be seen 'cause no one is listening
So I get louder and bigger instead
I spent a lifetime blaming celery
When all I wanted was to be fed

I'm sorry, Dear Celery, let's start over
We have a lifetime to heal.
It's not food, but love that I need
It should be in every meal

My weight and body dysmorphia issues are a direct connection to the sexual abuse and trauma I experienced in my youth. These issues are something I continuously work on. I am very proud of all I have accomplished, yet there are so many layers to this healing that I am still uncovering. I use my experiences and knowledge to help others work through their own recovery, and this in turn helps me to continue on my journey as well.

Permission Slip

Please take the time now to fill out this slip for yourself.

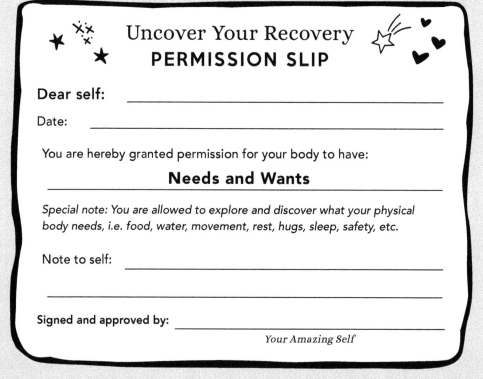

Uncover Your Recovery
PERMISSION SLIP

Dear self: _____

Date: _____

You are hereby granted permission for your body to have:

_____ **Needs and Wants** _____

Special note: You are allowed to explore and discover what your physical body needs, i.e. food, water, movement, rest, hugs, sleep, safety, etc.

Note to self: _____

_____

Signed and approved by: _____

Your Amazing Self

Invitation/Challenge

Take advantage of this opportunity: Write something that you found meaningful or significant from this chapter.

Ann's List BE KIND
to yourself

- [ ] Breathe
- [ ] Sleep, rest, take a nap
- [ ] Drink water
- [ ] Eat nourishing food
- [ ] Take a break from social media
- [ ] Shut off phone
- [ ] Ask for a hug
- [ ] Drink a cup of tea or coffee
- [ ] Watch a funny movie
- [ ] Laugh out loud
- [ ] Spend time in a garden
- [ ] Go to the library
- [ ] Stay in your pj's all day
- [ ] Take a bath or shower
- [ ] Purge old socks and underwear
- [ ] Go for a drive
- [ ] Get fresh air
- [ ] Go to the park
- [ ] Go to the beach
- [ ] Ask for support
- [ ] Go to the mountains
- [ ] Read a book

- [ ] Stretch
- [ ] Watch the sunrise or sunset
- [ ] Light a candle
- [ ] Give yourself a foot massage
- [ ] Have breakfast for dinner
- [ ] Compliment yourself
- [ ] Watch funny animal videos
- [ ] Take yourself out to eat
- [ ] Doodle, color, or draw
- [ ] Sing out loud
- [ ] Listen to birds
- [ ] Go for a bike ride
- [ ] Star gaze
- [ ] Buy a new pillow
- [ ] Buy yourself flowers
- [ ] Go for a walk
- [ ] Watch an old movie
- [ ] Go to a museum
- [ ] Go for a swim
- [ ] Pet a pet
- [ ] Practice gratitude
- [ ] Walk in the rain
- [ ] Get a massage or facial

MAURA'S MESSAGE FROM SPIRIT

The Clouds told me a story today.

If you were a Cloud you'd realize,
You don't care what people think when they look at you.
You are beautiful,
You keep changing shape,
You even change color.
You move with the wind,
You keep on going.
You know that every person that looks at you
Sees something different.
They are not right or wrong.
What they see, is about them.
Not about you.

You. You are a Cloud.

CHAPTER 8

Healing Tools to Consider

"What you make of your life is up to you.
You have all the tools and resources you need.
Your answers lie inside of you."

- DENIS WAITLEY

Are you still with us? Have you made it this far? We are proud of you. Let's find what resonates for you. It's your life you get to pick. So let's open our awareness to possibilities of utilizing more tools to heal. When we limit ourselves we create stagnation. When we choose, we create empowerment.

When we embark on a healing journey, we tend to think that we are going to use our mind to get through it. This is not the case as we've pointed out so many times along the way. Our minds are just one part of the healing journey. We have two other places to work with as well, our body and our spirit. Below we share ideas that incorporate the body, mind, and spirit.

Throughout the book we have talked about sensation and noticing our bodies through our senses and our feelings. This is all well and good, but we also need to *move* our physical bodies, we need to *nourish* our spiritual selves, and we need to *consciously look* at our personal thoughts. There are endless ways to explore and find what fits for you. Let's take a look again at how adverse events affect us and how emotions and responses get stuck in the body.

An example looks like this: we are young, maybe five or six, we are angry at someone. We hold our breath in our anger. We storm away, we are told it's not okay to be mad. In that one moment of breath holding, in that one moment of our feelings not being honored we've stopped the free flow of energy in our body. Our physical body constricts, our mind can create a perception and our spirit can be let down. Using this example of anger, if this repeats over and over for a long time, and we respond the same way each time, this creates an unhealthy pattern that affects body, mind, and spirit. This can also happen with other types of unresolved and unprocessed emotions.

When patterns like these get stuck, we need to move them and process them. The only way to move them is with action. You can't move stuck energy by thinking about it. You have to actually physically move your body.

> **Ann:** When I was in the beginning stages of therapy a lot of unresolved anger started showing up. One of the ways I started to process this anger was going to the local park and swinging on the swings. It got me into my body with the process of pumping my legs, I was out in the fresh air and releasing the pent-up, stuck energy and emotion of anger. This went on for a period of about two weeks and created a much-needed healthy outlet to process my emotions.

Creating a toolbox for movement and activity is very personal. What works for one person might not work for another. The idea though is to pick something that resonates with you, and then make a practice of it. We will give you a list of things to choose from and you can see which of those resonate for you or you can find something else. Some of you might have physical limitations, some may have time constraints, some may feel that they have no creativity, and some people just feel like they can't move at all. Let's honor all of that as well. We need to make the process accessible to ourselves so we can feel safe and supported.

Remember this, the only difference between stumbling blocks and stepping stones is how you use them.

As long as we don't let setbacks keep us from moving forward, we remain unstoppable.

The following is a list of tools, ideas, and suggestions for you to consider in creating your own new tool box.

Writing

The act of writing is not new in the world of expression. Usually, it's one of the first things that a therapist or support person might tell you to do. The cool thing about writing is that your hand is related to the heart. This is a powerful connection. The very act of moving your arm and allowing your pen to write is a really great way to release emotions.

Here's a few ways to work with words and writing.

Working with your curiosity, perhaps you've discovered a word for your feelings. An example could be frustration. Write the word frustration down. Let that be your prompt. And then without a lot of thought just let yourself write about all the ways that you feel frustrated. There's a difference between being frustrated and being angry so be mindful of that fact. Stay with the emotion of the frustration. If anger arises then make that a new prompt. Same with positive emotions and feelings, such as love, and gratitude.

It might be difficult in the beginning but just let your pen flow. If you're writing about frustration, let situations past and present come out and let the pen be your guide. This might take practice. Sometimes writing out our feelings can feel uncomfortable. If you are in a situation where you wouldn't want someone to find your writings, there's another practice you can use.

Doodling

Doodle writing and doodle journaling are a real thing. Instead of a pen, you can use any instrument, chalk, markers, crayons, or pencils. This practice can be used when the emotions are difficult, or writing does not seem to flow or resonate. Take your writing tool and allow yourself to start doodling. You can talk out loud or to yourself or allow your hand to move on the paper in whatever way it wants as you are mentally or verbally expressing. The idea of doodling is not putting words out into the universe, it's just allowing things that might not have words to be expressed in a different way. This is very powerful. This is also great in situations when you live with others or feel vulnerable in some way. Example, if you are a young person and you're dealing with your emotions around your parents, you can have a full journal of doodles which will have released a whole lot of tension and emotions but still retain your privacy.

Singing

Do you love to sing? Or do you think you can't sing? Singing and using our voice is one of the most powerful things we can do to heal ourselves. Music and sound are such powerful and vibrational healers. When you think about music you know that there are different songs that make you feel happy, sad, angry, or joyful. Music, singing, and dancing are some amazing ways to move energy.

Singing is related to the throat. This avenue has everything to do with our ability and our right to speak, and our right to be heard. These things are not always supported by our families of origin. This is where a lot of us get stuck and do not use our voice. A great way to use singing is to find songs that evoke emotion. If you are feeling sad, find the saddest song you know. *Listen* to it and sing. Or let your body move to the sound of the song. If you feel like just rocking or swaying, *allow that*. Let your body *feel* the sadness. Let your body *move*. Let yourself dance. Let yourself sing. Maybe you don't sing, maybe you just hum. Experiment with this. For a lot of people this can take practice. Practice, not to be "better," practice to be FREE.

Chanting also falls under this category. Chanting has been used for centuries by all different cultures. Chanting is a way of expressing ourselves and at the same time giving honor to a higher power. For instance, Gregorian chants are cool. If you have no idea what that means check it out online. It's an ancient art of chanting, with roots steeped in religion in the Catholic Church. This might feel uncomfortable for some people if religion is something you are recovering from. But it can be really comforting to listen and move to. Be curious about it.

In Buddhism specifically, chanting is a connection to the Divine Source. It is used as means to connect to Spirit for comfort and healing. In the yoga tradition it is the same way. Chanting and mantra repetition are utilized to help support people in their quest to find peace. A specific mantra that is believed to be universal is *So Hum*. These two words, when used together are loosely defined as *I am that,* or I am part of all that is. Which when we get right down to it, we truly are all one.

Painting, Art Projects, and Hobbies

Painting and art projects play a huge role in healing. Many art therapists bring all different kinds of mediums to help their clients. Some might use clay, paints, coloring, or other types of art projects to aid their clients in working out their challenges without having to use words. In Ann's own healing recovery, she was grateful to have worked with an art therapist early on. A lot of markers and coloring were used as a means to connect to the feelings that were not reachable with words. Again, like the other action tools, you don't need to be an artist to do this work. You can just get some markers, crayons, paints, clay, etc. and allow yourself to create anything, without even worrying about what the project might become.

We have offered workshops together, using mandalas and coloring. We would use the same mandala for everyone and the difference in the color scheme that people would pick was so telling in what was happening in their lives. It was amazing. This is a useful tool. Additionally, using Play-Doh, kinetic sand or clay is a great way for anyone to work through their feelings. Painting and arts and crafts tap into a whole deeper place in the nervous system, helping us move energy.

Did you have any hobbies or crafts that you loved in your childhood that you abandoned, or you miss and can't find the time? What are you interested in? Knitting, pottery, glass work, woodworking, jewelry making, art, anything you could do with your hands. It all ties back into your heart when you are working with your hands.

Walking

Walking is a simple and easy way to move our bodies. But for some people this might not be an easy process. There might be physical limitations that preclude you from walking. A different form of movement might be necessary for you. However, if you do have the ability to walk and haven't done it in a while that's okay too. Take it easy and go slow. *There's no winning in walking.* If you haven't been mobile for whatever reason, start easy. Possibly walk out the front door for as many steps that feel comfortable and come back. It is a great beginning. We can start to change our mindset when it comes to movement. Just because someone else walks five miles a day doesn't mean that you have to. Walking to the end of the block or walking upstairs is just as significant.

The idea of walking for movement can also have intention around it. For example, maybe you have some frustration or perhaps you've been feeling some sadness. An idea could be to take your walk with the sole intention of allowing yourself to feel that frustration or sadness and release it. This would be intentional walking. Something to get curious about. There is no one-size-fits-all action plan for healing. Find what resonates for you.

Running

Are you running? Running is one of the most profound ways for a lot of people to get rid of tension and stress. If you're one of those people that can make running a new project and action step, that's great. Running really gets the body's circulatory system moving, thereby expending energy. This is an activity that can help you move stuck energy and help create a self-care routine. Running is not for everyone.

> **Ann:** I for one am not a runner. I've tried with no success. I've honored that for myself. I used to have shame around running because my brothers were runners, and my father was a track coach. It was almost as if I was failing in some way that running wasn't a thing for me. It's taken me a long time to let go of that. I found other activities that suit my body type better than running. We need to find those activities that support us and resonate with us individually. Running just because your friends or your family say you should, isn't healthy, especially if you hate every minute of it. Find what works for you.

Yoga

Yoga can sometimes be confusing for many people. There's a lot of misinformation around this practice. Some myths are that you need to be flexible, it's a workout, it brings you to enlightenment, it's a religion, you can only practice on a mat, all teachers are the same, and that it's only about your physical body.

These things couldn't be further from the truth.

Yoga is not just about flexibility; it is not a religion or any of the above. Finding the right yoga teacher and yoga practice is a key. Yoga can meet you right where you are, if you have physical challenges, you're a beginner, or you can't get on the floor, etc. There are many styles and practices of yoga that you can try. Yoga can be *accessible* to all and every size body.

What is also great about yoga is that it is considered to be a self-healing practice. It can help us create stability throughout our healing journey. Yoga poses can sometimes be challenging. Practicing yoga can often create more balance and flexibility. It can help create a steady mind when working through our emotional, physical, and spiritual bodies. Researching, locating, and taking the right class can be very supportive for body, mind, and spirit.

QiGong/Tai Chi

These two practices are steeped in 5,000 years of tradition. QiGong and Tai Chi are somewhat like yoga, in that anyone can practice them regardless of their physical limitations. Any of the movements of these practices can be adapted for any body and everybody. These practices focus on breath control, slow body movements, and a whole system of wellness.

Swimming/Playing in the Water

Getting your body in water can be a very healing option. Water gives our bodies support, buoyancy, takes pressure off the bones and joints, and we become weightless in water. Swimming and other water activities are accessible to many people nowadays. Aside from oceans, lakes, and outdoor pools, there are also many indoor water options. Many gyms, and local YMCAs have pool accessibility offering water aerobics and other water related classes. Float tanks, hot tubs, and whirlpool soaks are also great options. Water has a powerful and soothing effect that can benefit most everyone.

Nature

The magic of nature is available to everyone. There is a bounty of choices. Maybe you live near the beach, a park, the mountains, or a lake. Maybe you have a tree outside your window, or you are somewhere where you can see the sky, the moon, or the stars. Trees, plants, and flowers can teach us so much about resilience. Nature supports our senses. The smells, sounds, sights, tastes, and the ability to touch our outdoor surroundings. There are studies that show it can lower our blood pressure, help us get grounded, and reduce stress. One of the best parts about being in nature is that it doesn't judge us, it asks nothing of us, just allows us to be.

What do you currently connect to in nature, or what has been calling you to connect? Maura loves thunderstorms, lightning, and rain. Ann loves the sun, the beach, and trees. What about you? What are your likes and dislikes about nature?

Breathing

Do you ever think about your breathing or how your breath actually works? Are you breathing correctly? Most of us take the gift of breathing for granted. Our breathing is truly miraculous. There are countless breathing techniques available, and you can research them online. Here's an invitation. Right now, turn your awareness to your own breath. Sit up a little straighter, pay attention to your inhale and exhale. Your shoulders may drop away from your ears a bit, you may notice a sense of calm in your body. Get curious, what else can you notice? Can you deepen that inhale and your exhale a bit. Does your breath feel shallow or deep? On your next exhale, make an audible sound like a sigh. Do that a few times and be curious about what you notice. Slowing our breathing down can help reduce anxiety and stress. Mindful breathing techniques can be such an effective tool to add to your toolbox.

Meditation, Prayer, Mindfulness

There's so much attention on meditation these days that it can be hard to figure out where to start. You don't need to buy anything. You don't need a special cushion, a special room, incense, candles, etc. What you do need is a place to sit, even if it is in your car. Meditation simply is the invitation to become more aware of your breath. This breath awareness can be the start to quieting your racing mind. We allow our breath to become the main focus. The purpose of meditation is not to stop our thoughts, it's to slow them down and detach from them. This detachment can allow more clarity and calmness. Allowing the focus to shift from our mind to our breath is a practice. Start with just one minute a day.

There are many forms of meditation. Prayer, guided meditation, connecting to nature, breath awareness, and mindfulness to name a few. Explore which methods work for you. Meditation is about practice. The more you practice the easier it becomes. Since it's not the length of time that is important, start anywhere. There are so many apps available to support you, you don't have to do it alone. This practice can change your life.
Do not Meditate while driving. 🙂

Sports

There are more sports than we can possibly list. Sports are such a great outlet. Thinking back, was there a sport that you were drawn to in your childhood. Is there something you are interested in now? It's true that not everyone is interested in participating in sporting activities. However, there are many adult groups available for you to get involved with. If you ran in high school for instance, there may be a running group in your neighborhood now. Pickleball is the newest craze and can be played by almost anyone. Maybe you might want to pick up a basketball again or go to the batting cages, but you have so many negative thoughts around it that you are missing all the fun and benefits that sports can offer. Such as the many health benefits, physical strength, flexibility, mobility, increased endorphins, decreased depression and anxiety, outlet for processing emotions, social connection, and many more advantages. Be curious, be aware, and find something that suits you.

Connecting with Animals

Animals, the most comforting, supportive, and non-judgmental creatures. We apologize to those of you that have animal allergies. We both know the value of the healing ability of our animal friends. Maura loves dogs and goats; Ann loves cats and dogs. What's your favorite animal? If you can't have a real one, can you have a stuffed one? Maura used to have 400 teddy bears, now she has just one, her original Red Teddy.

In whatever way, if you are able to connect with animals, we encourage you to do so. Their powerful presence, support, and unconditional love is boundless.

The Best Medicine is: Humor, Play, Laughter, and Gratitude

Besides nothing, what else have you tried? If you have been sitting around doing nothing for your own healing, this might be a great place to start. Both of our families of origin use humor as a trauma response. We both use humor still. While sometimes off-putting and possibly inappropriate, it still has its benefits. When was the last time you laughed out loud? If it hasn't been recent, you need to watch *Zootopia* or any comedy. We watched *Zootopia* during the writing of this book. The lines of humor in this movie were brilliant and thought-provoking. It helped us create some relaxation we desperately needed. It's time to explore. Find a funny movie, listen to or find some favorite comedians to follow.

Life can be challenging, this we know. But finding humor and fun is not only allowed but it is strongly recommended. Maybe it's time to go to a comedy club or schedule some play time with a friend. As adults we tend to think *playing* isn't productive and even think it's childish, but nothing could be further from the truth. Playing is a significant form of healing. What types of games do you like? Do you play any now? If your family wasn't into games, can you find one now that you might enjoy? Here's just a few that we enjoy; Uno, Mantis Shrimp, LCR (left center right), Banana Grams, Mexican Train, Boggle, Heads Up, Farkle, Pictionary, and Charades. Ann's family plays croquet, while this can be a fun family and friend game, it also has side effects because of its competitive nature, (just ask her relatives). Ha. Find what resonates for you.

As you can see, these are some of the tools that we have utilized in our healing journey, and we are now asking you to consider some of yours. We have also added our lists of gratitudes on the following pages. What are some combinations of tools and gratitudes that resonate for you? Add your own. This is your life; you get to choose. Maybe in your uncovering you remember a childhood pastime that you loved, playing the guitar, riding a bike, writing poetry, tap dancing, swimming, knitting/crocheting, etc. See if any of these still light a spark and try them again. The sky is the limit to what is available. It's time to create your own toolbox of healing.

Permission Slip

Please take the time now to fill out this slip for yourself.

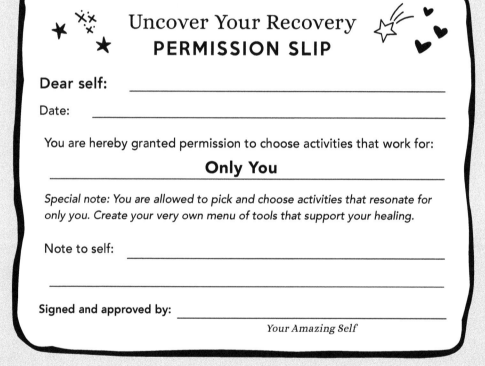

★ ✦✦ ★ ✦

Uncover Your Recovery
PERMISSION SLIP

Dear self: _____

Date: _____

You are hereby granted permission to choose activities that work for:

_____ **Only You** _____

Special note: You are allowed to pick and choose activities that resonate for only you. Create your very own menu of tools that support your healing.

Note to self: _____

_____

Signed and approved by: _____

Your Amazing Self

Invitation/Challenge

Take advantage of this opportunity: Write something that you found meaningful or significant from this chapter.

Ann's Gratitude List

- [ ] Sun
- [ ] Moon
- [ ] Stars
- [ ] Breath
- [ ] Family
- [ ] Trees
- [ ] Flowers
- [ ] Birds
- [ ] Cats
- [ ] Dogs
- [ ] Summer smells of rain
- [ ] Fall smells of leaves
- [ ] Spring smells of flowers blooming
- [ ] Winter smells of fires burning
- [ ] Travel
- [ ] My Nonna
- [ ] Indoor plumbing
- [ ] Water in every way
- [ ] The beach
- [ ] Seashells
- [ ] Rocks
- [ ] Animals of all kinds
- [ ] Angels and Saints
- [ ] The Divine Mother
- [ ] The Divine Father
- [ ] Technology
- [ ] Friends
- [ ] Cars
- [ ] Pens and pencils
- [ ] Paper to draw and write
- [ ] Smiles
- [ ] Babies laughter

- [ ] Music in all ways
- [ ] Body movement
- [ ] All the senses
- [ ] Love and kindness
- [ ] Lightness
- [ ] Darkness
- [ ] Constellations
- [ ] The galaxy
- [ ] Mountains
- [ ] All of nature
- [ ] Toothpaste
- [ ] Dental Floss
- [ ] Health
- [ ] People that care
- [ ] People that challenge me
- [ ] Freedom
- [ ] Divorce
- [ ] Food of all kinds
- [ ] Holidays
- [ ] New journal
- [ ] Pillows
- [ ] Yoga
- [ ] air-conditioning
- [ ] Heat
- [ ] Grass
- [ ] Lipstick
- [ ] Healthcare
- [ ] Sunrise
- [ ] Sunset
- [ ] Ritual
- [ ] Prayer
- [ ] Reiki

Maura's Gratitude List

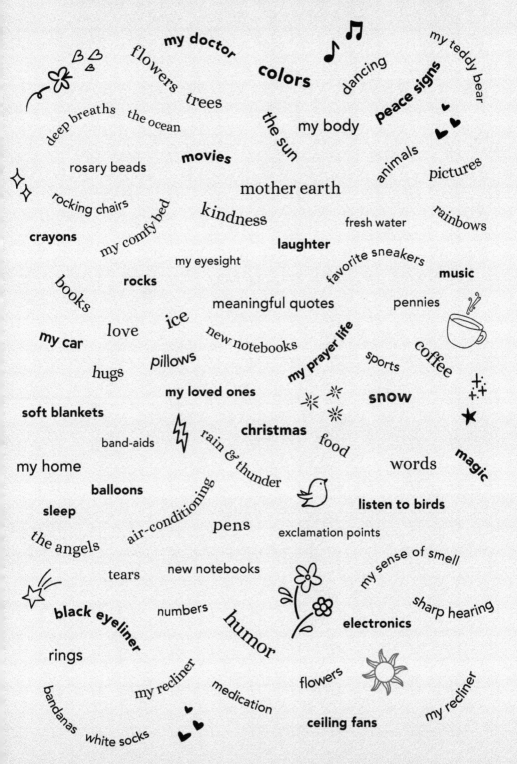

CHAPTER 9

Resources, Favorite Quotes, and Poems That Helped Us Along the Way

In this chapter you will find many resources, quotes, and poems that have supported us over the years, through our recovery, and still to this day. You will also find resources and contact information for organizations that may be supportive for you on your own recovery journey. We will end this chapter with our own personal writings to share with you.

We have found many programs helpful such as 12-step programs, retreats, holistic centers, and other online support groups. Many programs have been helping people in the recovery process for decades. You can do the research yourself and see what resonates for you. The beauty of the 12-step programs is that they have been adopted for most all behavior challenges, such as Gamblers Anonymous, Overeaters Anonymous, Workaholics Anonymous, etc... The way to determine what avenue of support is best for you is taking action steps and experiencing them for yourself. We are sharing our own stories below.

Ann's Story of 12-Step:

I belonged to SIA (Survivors of Incest Anonymous) back in the late 80s and 90s. This group is for women survivors of sexual abuse, regardless of whether the abuse was inside the family home, or outside the home with a non-family member. It still exists today. I went from attending to running a meeting for a few years. My personal take. It was exactly what it needed to be at the time for me. Then it wasn't and I needed to move on. I needed more than just talking and listening. I needed movement of my body, I needed to go deeper into what was underneath my thoughts. Every person that attends a meeting for whatever their reasons is to be applauded for their bravery and courage. To sit with others and bear witness to another person's story is sacred. I've learned though that I can talk my way around a lot of things, especially my feelings. I can intellectualize my trauma all day long. I can understand why I feel the way I do; I can understand my family of origin and do the whole dance. What was missing for me was the action of feeling my emotions and doing something with them. It's not the 12-steps' fault, it's not anyone's fault that they miss the mark for some people. We constantly evolve and so do programs, businesses, institutions, etc.

Mental Health evolves all the time. CBT or Cognitive Behavioral Therapy was thought to be the only way to heal, some think it still is. Maybe you are working with a therapist, and this is the method they use. That's great. My question always is though, are you able to feel your feelings and do something with the sensations that those feelings evoke in your physical, visceral body? My personal experience has taught me that when I'm activated by someone or something, I feel it in my body and no amount of me talking myself out of it is going to help. I need to acknowledge where I feel and then move it in some physical way.

The SIA program was profound for me. I learned so much about myself and others that was so beneficial. Have you ever tried a program like a 12-step? If you haven't can you be curious about why? Allow yourself some time to reflect on this idea. See what resonates. It might be just the thing you need to get you going, or not. Your choice now. You choose what works, no one else.

Maura's Story of 12-Step:

"Al-Anon is a mutual support program for people whose lives have been affected by someone else's drinking. By sharing common experiences and applying the Al-Anon principles, families and friends of alcoholics can bring positive changes to their individual situations, whether or not the alcoholic admits the existence of a drinking problem or seeks help."

One of the gifts I have learned in Al-Anon is giving the addict room and dignity to make their own choices. Not enabling. Not trying to fix. Not trying to cure. Not trying to change them. The only person we can change is ourselves. We hear this over and over in life. There is a lot of addiction in my family. Alcohol, drugs, food, etc. We each come to our own healing in our own way and in our own time.

Al-Anon continues to help me learn how to cope with the challenges of someone else's "using." I have found healthier ways to respond to these challenges. My understanding has grown tremendously. I have had to work on my boundary issues, both healthy and unhealthy ones, and I am still working on these today. I have learned that addiction is a family disease. Not everyone in the family is ready or even able to look at this unhealthy dynamic. Since we are each in charge of our own lives and our own reactions, I have had to examine *my* feelings about all of this. It is certainly multi-layered. Being angry, sad, and disappointed in family members is natural, but continuing to act from the place of that anger and disappointment is unhealthy and can even create more damage.

I started the healing process with curiosity of the entire scenario, first identifying my feelings, and then learning how to cope with and express those feelings in a healthy way. Being able to communicate them, attending Al-Anon meetings, reading supportive literature, praying and asking for help, are all tools I am using. With time, things have shifted. I have felt relief and even found a lot of serenity. I really do take things one day at a time. And this has made all the difference.

Here are the twelve steps of Alcoholics Anonymous:

The Twelve Steps:

1. We admitted we were powerless over alcohol—that our lives had become unmanageable.
2. Came to believe that a Power greater than ourselves could restore us to sanity.

3. Made a decision to turn our will and our lives over to the care of God as we understood Him.
4. Made a searching and fearless moral inventory of ourselves.
5. Admitted to God, to ourselves, and to another human being the exact nature of our wrongs.
6. Were entirely ready to have God remove all these defects of character.
7. Humbly asked Him to remove our shortcomings.
8. Made a list of all persons we had harmed, and became willing to make amends to them all.
9. Made direct amends to such people wherever possible, except when to do so would injure them or others.
10. Continued to take personal inventory and when we were wrong promptly admitted it.
11. Sought through prayer and meditation to improve our conscious contact with God as we understood Him, praying only for knowledge of His will for us and the power to carry that out.
12. Having had a spiritual awakening as the result of these steps, we tried to carry this message to alcoholics, and to practice these principles in all our affairs.

Anonymity is the spiritual foundation of all our Traditions, ever reminding us to place principles before personalities.

The Twelve Traditions:

1. Our common welfare should come first; personal recovery depends upon AA unity.
2. For our group purpose there is but one ultimate authority—a loving God as He may express Himself in our group conscience. Our leaders are but trusted servants; they do not govern.
3. The only requirement for AA membership is a desire to stop drinking.
4. Each group should be autonomous except in matters affecting other groups or AA as a whole.
5. Each group has but one primary purpose—to carry its message to the alcoholic who still suffers.

6. An AA group ought never endorse, finance, or lend the AA name to any related facility or outside enterprise, lest problems of money, property, and prestige divert us from our primary purpose.
7. Every AA group ought to be fully self-supporting, declining outside contributions.
8. Alcoholics Anonymous should remain forever nonprofessional, but our service centers may employ special workers.
9. AA, as such, ought never be organized; but we may create service boards or committees directly responsible to those they serve.
10. Alcoholics Anonymous has no opinion on outside issues; hence the AA name ought never be drawn into public controversy.
11. Our public relations policy is based on attraction rather than promotion; we need always maintain personal anonymity at the level of press, radio, and films.

The Serenity Prayer by Reinhold Niebuhr

God, grant me the Serenity
To accept the things I cannot change . . .
Courage to change the things I can,
And Wisdom to know the difference.
Living one day at a time,
Enjoying one moment at a time,
Accepting hardship as the pathway to peace.
Taking, as He did, this sinful world as it is,
Not as I would have it.
Trusting that He will make all things right
if I surrender to His will.
That I may be reasonably happy in this life,
And supremely happy with Him forever in the next.
Amen.

Below we have listed our favorite sayings, poems, and blessings that have spoken to us in one way or another. We believe that poetry, writings, and quotes from others can all be supportive tools in *Uncovering Your Recovery.* It helps us navigate our lives when someone else's work resonates with us. Their words can help us feel less lonely and isolated, leading us to feeling less alone. Our compilation is not exhaustive, we add to it all the time. We invite you to be curious and uncover your own.

Some of Ann's Favorite Poems and Quotes

 The first two sentences have always resonated with me. It gives me permission to release myself from shame.

Mary Oliver – *Wild Geese*

You do not have to be good.
You do not have to walk on your knees….

 I first read this poem in 2006. It changed my life completely. I share this poem with everyone I know.

Mary Oliver - *The Journey*

One day you finally knew
What you had to do, and began….

 Donna's poetry has a way of getting right to the point of what I sometimes have no words for.

Donna Ashworth – *I Wish I Knew*

I wish I knew, from the start,
that self-esteem is a home grown virtue.

John speaks always to my heart with every one of his writings. His deep wisdom and compassion for others is in every word he writes.

John O'Donohue - *A Blessing for Suffering*

May you be blessed in the holy names of those, Who, without you knowing it, Help to carry and lighten your pain.

John O'Donohue - *For Someone Awakening To The Trauma of His or Her Past*

For everything under the sun there is a time.

 This poem has resonated with me since about 1995 when I found it in the book, *The Courage to Heal.*

Portia Nelson - Autobiography in Five Short Chapters - Chapter 1 - I walk down the street.

 John, like so many others has a way with words that truly resonate the feelings that are hard to express.

John Roedel - *The Anatomy of Peace*
(formerly titled *"How to Live With My Body"*)

my brain and
heart divorced
a decade ago
over who was
to blame about
how big of a mess
I have become

We must be willing to let go of the life we planned so as to have the life that is waiting for us.
  - Joseph Campbell

The topic of compassion is not at all religious business; it is important to know it is human business, it is a question of human survival.
  - Dalai Lama XIV

There is a light in this world, a healing spirit more powerful than any darkness we may encounter.
  - Mother Theresa

To be brave, we don't need to be free from fear, we just need a purpose bigger than fear.
  - Bhagavad Gita

Some of Maura's Favorite Quotes

A journey of a thousand miles begins with a single step.
  - Lao Tzu

As you start to walk on the way, the way appears.
  - Rumi

Almost everything will work again if you unplug it for a few minutes, including you.
  - Anne Lamott

Hope is the grace that comes in and helps you start breathing.
  - Caroline Myss

Don't let someone who gave up on their dreams talk you out of going after yours.
  - Zig Ziglar

Not all those who wander are lost.
  - J.R.R. Tolkein

If you are going through hell, keep going.
  - Winston Churchill

Storms make trees take deeper roots.
  - Dolly Parton

When we meet real tragedy in life, we can react in two ways – either by losing hope and falling into self-destructive habits, or by using the challenge to find our inner strength.
  - Dalai Lama

Nothing is permanent in this world, not even our troubles.
- Charlie Chaplin

Sometimes you get the best light from a burning bridge.
- Don Henley

You might have to fight a battle more than once to win it.
- Margaret Thatcher

Many of life's failures are people who did not realize how close
they were to success when they gave up.
- Thomas A. Edison

If you can't fly then run, if you can't run then walk, if you can't walk then
crawl, but whatever you do you have to keep moving.
- Martin Luther King

The only place success comes before work is in the dictionary.
- Vince Lombardi

Sometimes we think too much and feel too little.
- Charlie Chaplin

Weeds are flowers too, once you get to know them.
- Eeyore

That's the trouble with earth, we don't talk anymore. We've all become a
bunch of unopened love letters.
- Erin Van Vuren

The truth is, most of us discover where we are headed when we arrive.
- Bill Watterson / *Calvin & Hobbes*

I learned a long time ago the wisest things I can do is be on my own side.
- Maya Angelou

Sometimes the bravest and most important thing you can do is just show up.
  - Brene Brown

Life is a great big canvas throw all the paint you can on it.
  - Danny Kaye

Respect all the work you've done.
  - Danielle LaPorte

You are never too old for anything.
  - Betty White

Have faith in the unlimited, loving power of the universe.
  - Louise Hay

I saw the angel in the marble and carved until I set him free.
  - Michelangelo

Unconditional love does not mean unconditional tolerance.
  - Anonymous

Laughter is the fireworks of the soul.
  - Josh Billings

Short List of Resources

National Alliance on Mental Health nami.org

National Suicide Prevention Lifeline: Dial 988 988lifeline.org

Crisis Text Line: 741-741 crisistextline.org

Onsite experienceonsite.com

Survivors of Incest Anonymous siawso.org

Trauma Healing - Somatic Experiencing Practitioner information and locator traumahealing.org

Substance Abuse and Mental Health Services Administration, SAMHSA's National Helpline samhsa.gov/find-help/national-helpline

Alcoholics Anonymous aa.org

Narcotics Anonymous na.org

Overeaters Anonymous oa.org

National Eating Disorders Association nationaleatingdisorders.org

Gamblers Anonymous gamblersanonymous.org/ga

National Domestic Violence Hotline thehotline.org

Connect with the Authors
Ann Merli: cardinalwaywellness.com
Maura Bertotti: maurabertotti.com
Facebook Group: Uncover Your Healing

Writings by Maura Bertotti and Ann Merli

Maura Bertotti - *Can I Love You Sober*

If only my love was enough
and I could help you see your light

If there was a way for me to save you
I'd help you with this fight

But that is not the way it works
No one else can ease your pain

With the demons of addiction
The scars stubbornly remain

They are there, on you, on me
You don't just hurt your self
I feel the struggle you live with
I pray that I could help

If I could love you to sobriety
My love would be the fix
Instead of demon substances
That are an empty, aching mix

A dark and driving force
At the bottom of a well
A place of utter darkness
A living, painful hell

If all my love was medicine
To heal and make you whole
I'd use it in a heartbeat
You wouldn't need to sell your Soul

You wouldn't feel alone in this,
as it tears you apart
If I could love you sober
I'd do it with all my heart

Ann Merli - *The Miracle of Breath*

When I come into my breath and look at it with a new lens, it always
restores me.
Breathe in and out, miracle in every breath.
Breathe in and out, miracle in every inhale.
Breathe in and out, miracle in every exhale.
Breath a miracle of still being here with opportunity.
To feel sad, to feel happy to open our eyes to new beginnings.
Breath a miracle of still being here with kindness.
To family and friends, to ourselves, to strangers
Breath a miracle of still being human.
With choices, with questions, with emotions unexpressed
Breathing a miracle that we take for granted.

Our passed loved ones would say, take a breath for me as I no longer
have one.
Our passed loved ones would say, be kinder to yourself, it's not worth it
in the end.
Our passed loved ones would say, breathe, walk, go out in nature, take in
the beauty.
Our passed loved ones would say, breathe for me and change what we
couldn't.
Our passed loved ones would say they are sorry for any transgressions,
breathe into your life.

The inhale a miracle when we arrive, the exhale a miracle when we leave. All the while we are here, we can use the ebb and flow to heal ourselves. Allowing inhale to nourish restriction and contraction, allowing exhale to release restriction and contraction.

We are always looking for a miracle outside of ourselves, we are a miracle. Our breathing is a miracle that is connection to our inner knowing amazing self.

Our breathing is the connection to Source, God, the infinite Universe. Filled with our humanity of being part of the bigger whole, our breath is what unites us to all living things. It is our connection to otherness. When all we see sometimes is difference, coming home to the breath reminds us that as long as we are here on our home planet Earth, we are not different than anyone else, the miracle of our breaths connects us all.

Breathe in and breathe out. Let the movement of your breath be your focus. One second, two seconds, three, four, five. Notice the inner sanctum of your physical temple of your body.

Every next inhale offers choice, every next exhale offers freedom.

Each one of us carries burdens, no two alike, our unique selves carrying our unique lived experiences into the world. The hardships, the guilt, the blame and shame, the joys, the loves, the beauty, all experienced through our uniqueness that our breath allows us to have.

Although our burdens can feel heavy and that no one will ever understand them, we are united in the miracle of our breath. When we can sit with someone in despair and match our breath to the rhythm of theirs, we are united in the miracle of breathing, of supporting without judgment.

One second at a time, one moment of the now of now is sometimes all we have. Follow the breath, notice the breath, let the outside slip away, come back to the inside, the miracle of you. Your unique self that offers to the world your unique experiences that might just help another, that might just change a past, that might just change the future. Inside is the miracle, the language of our love connection to Source that knows us and experiences life through us.

Without our breath here in the now, Source can't have experiences through our unique lens of life. Source needs these experiences, the harsh, the cruel, the sad, the joys, the love, the awe. Source needs them to have more compassion, to have more kindness, to keep the miracle of all of us still moving through the breath of hope. Learning, growing, falling down, up again, leaning in, shouting, singing, dancing, the mosaic of our life is a miracle that only the breath can give us.

Breathe, just breathe.

CHAPTER 10

Healing Journey Stories from Ann and Maura

We have written these stories to support you on your own healing path. We believe that it's helpful to know that you are never alone. This book and our stories are our hope and prayer that you can feel supported and safe enough to venture into your life with bravery and courage.

Ann's Story

From the beginning and throughout the book I mention a lot of my life story in my journal entries. As we have throughout the book, some things bear repeating. I tell my story to remind others that that through the kindness of others healing can be found.

In July of 1987, the month and year my father died, my life was altered in three ways. My first big death of someone close to me. No more secrets. My life will never be the same as it was before.

Sexual abuse is a life experience that no child should ever have to go through. Countless numbers of children do though at the hands of unhealthy people with a perversion toward children. It's a sickness, it wasn't my fault. There I said it. That one sentence that changed my life. Said by an adult friend, in a random conversation, who knew me when I was a young child.

My abuse was outside the home with a trusted family friend. Grooming was the tool used to create the havoc and chaos that would ultimately become my life for a very long time. The abuse shaped my life, my decisions, my behavior, every fiber of who I was and who I am today.

> **NOTE:** Grooming is a thing. It is the act of building a relationship, trust, and emotional connection with a child or person so that they can be manipulated, exploited, and abused. It's always used as a tactic to switch the blame from the perpetrator to the abused.

The adult friend who told me it wasn't my fault helped me find my amazing therapist. She specialized in art therapy and childhood trauma. I had started my healing journey. I was twenty-four. The first two years I attended therapy once a week, thereafter it changed and morphed as needed for the next six years. Through this therapy I came to use art, role play, and traditional Cognitive Behavioral Therapy (CBT). All of which were helpful and life-changing. At the request of my therapist, I also joined a Survivors of Incest Anonymous Group (SIA). Back in the 80's and early 90's, no one was talking about sexual abuse outside the home too much, but this group was inclusive and still is. This group was profound, and I learned so very much from every brave woman I came to know.

Some of my relationships during this time of therapy had to end. I divorced during this time, my relationship with my mother became strained, and I cut ties with some friends that were no longer healthy for me. This part was not easy. Having learned an early lesson, that I must have done something wrong for the abuse to happen, cutting ties and standing up for myself was not easy. Therapy and support gave me the tools to be brave and courageous and take care of me.

I married again at thirty, too hastily I need to add. Still so young and naive, thinking this one would be different and save me. I didn't realize yet that I needed to save myself. I was good, therapy for eight years taught me so much. I was still searching for the one, the person that would validate me. I thought this was the one. I stopped going to therapy. That decision did not age well. Two years into this marriage I knew it was a mistake. It took seven more years to leave. Eventually, toward the end of this marriage, I did go back to therapy, it helped to support my decision to save myself and get out.

From the time I was twenty-four till I got divorced for the second time at thirty-nine, I had been working through my childhood trauma in various ways. Although I left therapy for a time, I had been awakened into the world of alternative healing. I started my yoga journey, I read countless self-help books, looked for every external healing source I could find. I dabbled in different organized churches, thinking that would surely help. I learned a lot. I kept thinking about changing jobs, going back to school to be a nurse or a massage therapist. I wanted to help other people.

With two divorces behind me and feeling like I failed at relationships, embarrassed by this failure, there was a lot still going on in my life. I felt like I let my family down. Not only was I divorced once, I was divorced twice. At work there was a lot of teasing for my various name changes. In retrospect, at least I had the courage to leave, instead of staying in unhealthy relationships.

Even though I had logged countless therapy hours, there was still something wrong with me, at least, that's how I felt. I had a healthier outlook on life, could see some of my continued unhealthy behavior patterns and try to change them, although sometimes that didn't work. I repeatedly fell in the "what the hell am I doing here again?" hole.

As I shared in the beginning of the book, in 2006 I was fortunate to attend the "Learning to Love Yourself" program at Onsite in Cumberland Furnace, TN. Having no idea of what to expect this workshop and the subsequent path of healing changed the trajectory of my whole life after that. It was an immersive intense week of experiential therapy. In a group of ten people who didn't know each other, we worked through our traumas together, with role play, movement, yelling, screaming, and a whole lot of unconditional support. The most intense and healing experience that left me angry, finally. I say angry and finally because anger was never part of my awareness. In order to be good, so people would like me, I never got angry.

After Onsite, I got really angry. So angry that it was time to find an alternative to conventional Cognitive Behavioral Therapy (CBT). I found a Somatic Experiencing Practitioner (SEP), and this made all the difference in my healing then and continues to this day. CBT can help make sense of things in the mind, Somatic Experiencing (SE) takes it a step further and helps heal the body, influencing the mind and spirit. SE works on the sensation experiences in the body of old trauma and helps to release them in a gentle way, supporting the nervous system, which in turns helps heal the patterns that the mind holds. From 2006 until today I still see my SEP when I need to. The support, release, and clarity that comes from these sessions is profound.

In 2006 I also chose a different life partner to have a relationship with. Challenging as it was, we lived in two different states, it has been the best connection that I could ask for. We dated long distance for ten years, before marrying in 2015. In that time, we learned, grew, challenged, broke up, loved, laughed, and learned so much about each other. Our marrying in 2015 also gave me the permission I needed to leave my job of twenty-nine and a half years and move on to my current life. Relationships are never easy, although they can be the best spiritual practice we may ever encounter.

I come to this book today, humbled, and grateful. In writing this book there have been many challenges that Maura and I have both worked on. The writing experience of this book has taken us both to other depths of our own healing. We have done all the work contained in the chapters, and we continue every day. Being awake, aware, and full of curiosity has its drawbacks in a good way. I can never go back to having my head in the sand about my healing, I get to question everything I do, my behaviors and how they affect me and other people. It may not always feel great, it can feel lonely and uncomfortable. Overall though, the deeper connection to myself, Spirit, and those around me are the benefits of the hard work. In the heart of me, I feel more peace and calm, more grounded and supported.

The first step can be hard to take, our wounding runs deep, most of us have been mentally trying to figure it out for a long time. To get to the core though, we cannot separate the body, mind, and spirit. They need to heal together, not separately. We live in such an amazing time to have so many modalities to support us. Be kind and compassionate toward yourself first and foremost. Bravery and courage are your companions. Peace be yours.

Maura's Healing Journey

Growing up I was surrounded by a loving family and dear, close-knit friends. The one square mile neighborhood we roamed around in was much like a place from an old movie. Some blocks were safer than others, some were scary, and you learned to keep yourself surviving through the uncertainty. Times were challenging in a city that was plagued by political upheaval, poverty, gentrification, hard core warriors. Some of the toughest and bravest people I know are the ones I grew up with. Families surviving, thriving, hard-working, and religious.

Faith was a given. We prayed and went to church from the day we were born. And still we spent our teen years at dirt parks and rusty old piers down by the river. We lost many friends to the insidious disease of addiction. Such losses. So many broken hearts. I am beyond proud of many of my dear friends from my roots, who are in recovery today. Survivors, with deep stories of their own. All of us with bonds created through adversity and perseverance. Today, we take one day at a time because it is the only way to keep moving forward.

It is true that pain, loss, and disappointment have colored my world. The many losses I've experienced have truly shaped my life. Over the course of five decades, I have lost such significant, dear souls. Grief is a powerful sword that cuts sharply through joy and steals our peace. In my childhood, I experienced sexual abuse. Unfortunately, I also had some very emotionally abusive coaches and teachers. And thus, my coping mechanisms included an unhealthy relationship to my body and to food. Using food as an escape and a medicator, I created a lifestyle of dieting, binge eating, losing and gaining ridiculous amounts of weight. A lifetime of continuous struggle, it has been an exhausting and depressing battle. Only in very recent years have I made significant strides in my recovery.

Using the very tools and steps in this book that Ann and I have written, I have come to a place of healing. Healing is an ongoing process, but I no longer see it as a battle. I see it as a gift. There are so many lessons, both good and bad, and all of them are shaping my NOW.

In October of 2020, I discovered a program called Bright Line Eating. I gave up flour and sugar. I lost 160 pounds in two and a half years, and have since gained some of it back. The battle continues. I have lost and gained weight my entire life. Hundreds of pounds. I have to say the "losing" hasn't been the toughest part. My deepest work is continuing in the form of deep emotional work. Once upon a time my brother Kevin said to me, "Maura, who would you be if you weren't losing and gaining weight?"

Profound.

Profound especially because I didn't have an answer. I am finding out that answer now. Uncovering day by day. Realizing that "who I am" is a writer, a healer, a teacher; a sensitive and emotional person who loves simplicity in my life. Peace around food, around my body, and around acceptance does not come easily to me. There are good days and bad days. I am a work in progress . . . as we all are.

The death of my mother created a vast void in my heart and in my life that has affected me to this day. Over twenty-two years later, it has been the single most powerful loss I have ever had. It has led me on winding roads of expansion and knowledge, it has brought me to the depths of hell and darkness, and it has led me to the Blessings of Spirit and Light, all simultaneously.

In loss, I uncovered my new paths of Spirituality. For over twenty-two years, I've developed my intuitive gifts and I have shared them with others in Holistic Centers I opened at the Jersey Shore. Holding fairs, classes, events, seminars, and such. Teaching about psychic development, readings, angels, mediumship, healing, meditation, and so much more. Up until the Covid pandemic, I believed this would be my journey for the rest of my life. But like everyone, so much shifted during that crazy transitional time. Spirit led me away from that work for a bit to push me further into the *world of writing*. I know now it was a temporary design for my own healing. And now I am back to helping others with their own health and healing journey. Back to teaching Classes, doing Readings, holding Zooms, Channeling the Angels, sharing Hypnosis. We work virtually, as well as once again seeing some people in person. If Spirit so leads me to it, I will open another Holistic Center. But that remains to be seen. In the meantime, it has been so important to me to give people relief from their grief, to help them with their own struggles with this battle of food addiction, to bring them through their own personal Connections to Spirit, and to support their healing. Throughout my own extensive experiences, I bring to others the knowledge of what has and has not worked for me. I share the steps of healing that I have learned, and help identify the pitfalls and quicksand-traps along the way. It brings me great joy to give someone their own prescription for success, and to release them from the hell that has bound us to repeated cycles of exhausting battles. I want to continue to lead people into their personal freedom, as I am continuing to be led into mine.

As I've shared, I have battled weight issues for most of my entire life. Weight loss surgeries became popular in the 1990s and I have personally known hundreds of people who have experienced these surgeries over the past few decades. It was not something I considered. (Although many people over the years have asked me to do just that.) Even with well over one hundred pounds to lose, I did not think any of those surgeries would be a "fix" for me. Somehow I knew that my stomach itself was not the real problem. I always used to say that even if I wired my mouth shut I would still find a way to gain weight. That was my innate, deep-seeded belief.

I had so much to heal, so much to change, I knew surgery at that time was not going to benefit me. I have however always considered breast reduction surgery. Even though I have never had contributing factors such as having children, as I have never been pregnant, my breast size was absolutely a chronic issue for me. Due to losing and gaining literally hundreds of pounds over the years, that added immensely to the disproportionate size and density. This created more self-consciousness, and so much discomfort and physical pain. It was chronically intolerable. When your bra cup size is moving down the alphabet, from a double DD to letters H I J K , it becomes a quality-of-life issue. I knew it was time.

I explored, searched, and researched diligently on who and what would be the right fit for me to accomplish my new goals. My prayers, along with a friend's recommendation, brought me to my current doctor, Doctor Asaad Samra. Not only is he a phenomenal plastic surgeon, but he is also a wonderful human being. He and his family-practice have embraced me and have lovingly cared for me for over three years. I felt a soul connection to Dr.

Asaad as soon as I met him. We went through all the proper motions, consultations, and examinations, and scheduled my breast reduction surgery. I had zero fear. I felt as though I had waited so long for this day to come, and I met the exact right person to do it. The very morning of surgery I got on the scale, and I hit my first goal of losing one hundred pounds, that very morning! I was truly ecstatic. The surgery went wonderfully, and it remains the best medical decision I have ever made. It has authentically changed my life. This has been a whole new beginning, a new lease on life. A body that when healed, could exercise, could move through this world in different fitting clothes, could begin to see life in a whole new way. This has been the start of my ultimate goal. To shift my focus away from the never-ending cycle of losing and gaining weight, measuring myself in pounds and inches, and defining my self-worth based on changing clothes and bra sizes. My focus now has to be on healthy, vibrant foods, fun, engaging body movement, creative projects, and meaningful connections. Dr. Asaad has given me a new lease on life, and I am forever grateful to him. My new lifestyle has given me a new opportunity for long-term health.

My motto going forward has been **Healthy, Healthy, Strong and Wealthy.** Which reminds me of a poem I learned in high school, author unknown. It stuck with me immediately, I could repeat it as soon as I heard it and I have never forgotten it. I knew it was deep and vastly important. It has always spoken volumes to me.

The Clock of Life

The clock of life is wound but once
And no man has the power
To tell just when the hands will stop
At late or early hour
To lose ones wealth is sad indeed
To lose ones health is more
To lose ones soul is such a loss
That no man can restore

Wealth is important to a degree. Health is paramount to our quality of life. But our SOUL is what needs the most healing and connection of all. My goal now is to continue to uncover and discover what is next here on this life journey for me. And my ultimate wish is that you, the reader, find what it is you need for your own heart, body, mind, and soul. If the ocean, the earth, a spider, the trees, the fog, the rain, the rocks, or the clouds want to tell you a story, I hope you listen. I hope you are discovering how very special and miraculous you are. I believe in you. I hope as you uncover many things throughout these pages, you can also come to believe in yourself.

Acknowledgements

From Maura

There is not enough time or space to thank everyone properly.

- To our publisher, Jenn Young, thank you for believing in our project throughout its development and birth, it has been a true labor of Recovery for all of us. And to all the wonderful warrior women I met through this process.

- To my co-Author, Ann Merli, this is a journey we will never, ever forget. With so many memories made, tears cried, laughs created, there are no accurate words to capture this experience.

- For my many clients and students, thank you for also being my constant teachers as well. I appreciate all of you.

- For the special members of my Spiritual Community who, over these many years, have passed away. Thank you for touching my life with such significance.

- The many special friends and family, I cannot possibly name each one of you but you know who you are, and so do I. You have loved and supported me through the good times and the challenging times, I thank you sincerely.

- Special love to my nieces and nephews who have my whole heart, always and forever. You have no idea how much light you have brought into my life as you were each brought into this world and gave me the proud title of Aunt Maura.

- For my siblings, Kelly, Mark, and Kevin, Teachers come in many forms, you three have been a special kind of crazy-experience that only a family like ours could provide. I thank you for the life lessons, the roller coasters we are still on, and the love we share. There are many promises of peace and healing I still hold out hope for, as we grow and uncover our individual paths of recovery each and every day.

- To the following special and powerful people who have either saved, influenced, or changed my life in such profound ways. I offer you my sincerest gratitude, respect, and awe. Some of you are my Angels in Heaven, always watching over me. My other dear ones here below, we are still continuing our journey on this earth as there is more for us to do.

Lorraine Cutillo, Annmarie Gogliucci, Tracey Drayton, Debbie Fullam, Gloria Cutillo, my ASH Sisters, Sharon Fallo & my Hoboken Crew, Lisa Leidecker, Candra Savage, Pamela Meredith, Jessica Hoeverman, Adrienne Gammal, Sherry Robin Miller, Fayth Ellen Newell, Danielle Marggraf, my BLE Bayonettes, Doctor Asaad H. Samra, Amanda, Ashley, and the entire Samra Gang.

Please continue to Rest in Peace My Angels :
  My Grandmother, Mary Kneafsey Murray
  My Uncle, John A. Bertotti
  My Mother, Patricia Bridget McNamara
  My Father, Francis Xavier Bertotti
  My Dearest Mentor and Friend, Terry Labruno

I will always be overwhelmingly grateful to all of you as I share my heartfelt blessings and love. My heart is full.

And lastly, my deepest thanks to God and all the Angels, for without my faith, none of this would be possible.

Acknowledgements

From Ann

The acknowledgement for this book has been written in different ways over the past thirty plus years of my life. I always wanted to write a book, but I never knew how or when it would show up. I've started many books in my head, and some fragments handwritten in journals, on my computer, old USB drives. The acknowledgement always seemed easy in the above, in this book it's been the last thing I've written. It's real this time, this book will be published, the other thoughts and writings just for me. It's taken a lot to write from my heart, to be vulnerable.

The tears still fall silently every time I think about the night in 1987 that changed my life forever. I still don't know to this day what prompted the visit to my place of work, or the why, but I can say now, it was Divine intervention. When I heard the words "Annie, whatever happened to you when you were a little girl was not your fault," the world felt upside down and very surreal. When the conversation turned deeper, I felt exposed and vulnerable. The secret I had been asked to keep long ago, was now out. I'm forever indebted to you John C., you may never know that your act of courage and bravery that night saved a young girls life, mine. Thank you from every place in my heart. I use your words often when working with others that have been through the same pain and grief. I believe that just hearing them can be a balm to another's soul, righting a ship that had lost its anchor. Your words anchored me back to myself, allowed me to heal. It's taken thirty-seven years to be able to finally acknowledge you out loud. I am eternally grateful to you.

So many others to thank and acknowledge, how to fit them all in and in what order? Will anyone be offended if I leave them out, who should I leave out? Who should I put it? My ancestors, most recent and those that started my family from both sides. Thanks for showing up and giving me an opportunity to heal some old ancestral trauma and for sharing the wisdom of the things that needed to be carried on. Deepest gratitude to my Nonna Assunta Merli, her sweetness and kindness are the most heartfelt memories from my childhood. To my parents, Edith Diggory Merli and Nick Merli for everything you were and weren't as parents, it all served a purpose and I'm grateful that you had me last. My siblings, Chris Merli, Susan Merli, Stephen Merli, and Donna Merli Letizia, although perceptions of our past may differ, a silent thread of connection runs through each of us that can't be broken. Thank you to each of you from my deepest heart.

A special thank you goes out to my sister-in-law Theresa Merli; I've known you for almost my entire life. I'm grateful for your wit, wisdom, and overall presence in my life. To my nieces, nephews, and their significant others, for your unending support of your Aunt Annie in all the incarnations that you have witnessed. I love each of you to the deepest core of my being. My life would not have as much joy without each of you in it. Thanks to each of you for bringing your own children into the family. All my great nieces and nephews give me so much joy and hope. A special shout out to my cousins Sandy Antenori Zahner and Rick Merli, and their awesome spouses, your unending support and friendship means the world to my heart. Liz Musgrove, family through friendship always, thanks for all the support and your amazing organizational skills you bring to my life.

To all my teachers and mentors through the years. Special thanks to Ted Freeman, my boss for countless years, co-worker, mentor, friend he taught me always to see greatness and positivity in the darkest times of my life. Special thanks also to my teacher and friend, Anna Withrow who taught me the incredible value of the word curiosity. Thanks also to the 7:30 am check- in crew. Your support and lots of laughs help so much.

To my countless extended family and friends from childhood and till today, whether we see each other still or whether my memories of you are in my heart, thank you. My oldest friends from grade school and high school knew me during the time when my secret was still secret, the closest ones still know me today and have supported me through all of it with kindness and love. Special thanks to Gary Friedhoff and Cheri Witham for always just being there through it all. My closest circle of friends spans from north to south, from New Jersey to Florida and places in between. Thank you,

Acknowledgements

Kathy Paton sister/friend, for all your support, especially our impromptu late night talks of solving world problems. Thanks to you and Roy for your unending hospitality of giving me a home away from home. Bobbi Torres, thank you for being an amazing Spirit Momma. Your guidance and support through the years means the world to me. Barb Orgen, laughs and tears and all the in between thank you so much for the years of our friendship. Ginny Vigne, thanks for finding me at the yoga studio and becoming one of the best friends/sisters a girl could have. Shout-out to the Rhinelander, Wisconsin summer crew, especially Jamie Verley. This acknowledgment had its beginnings out on Lake Hildebrand alone in the blue kayak with just a pen and a journal. Your friendship, laughs, game playing, and food support are memories always inside of me. Thanks for accepting me right where I am.

To all my clients and students, thank you for making me always be a student first and teacher/practitioner second. Your willingness to allow me into the most vulnerable places in your life has been the honor of a lifetime. I always knew that I wanted to help others, but I never knew what that would look like in reality. All my training and hands on practice always leads me back to the Divine connection that happens when we work together. Thank you all for being in my life. I truly believe that serving others with unconditional support, love, and kindness is the key to healing, it was for me, and it always will be the basis of my working practices.

Gratitude to two of the best therapists someone could ever ask for, Barbara Paulsen from the beginning and Matthew Whaley through today. Without your insight and unconditional support, I would not be where I am today. Therapy is a thing, it's never a weakness to utilize this valuable support, it's powerful beyond measure.

To the Inspired Girl group, especially Jenn Tuma Young. Thank you for your support during the writing of this book. Editing and managing a co-author book has its challenges. Jenn and all the editors worked diligently to ensure our book met our combined vision and honored our uniquenesses. I'm extremely grateful.

My friend for life and co-author Maura Bertotti. We have been on this road together in many ways. Sometimes the same side of the road, sometimes next to each other, sometimes one behind the other. Sister, teacher, mentor, friend. Past lives, current lives, future lives, soul sisters to the core. We've been to hell and back again writing this book together. They say when you write a book, the content is usually what you are going through or have gone through. So many times, in writing I wanted to stuff all the emotions right back in, not feel any of them. We've cried, laughed, learned, and been frustrated so often in writing this book. It's been a heartfelt journey every step of the way. We have lived every chapter of this book together and separate, we worked through every ounce of the words written on these pages. We have indeed uncovered our recovery and uncovered our healing. At times it's been heart wrenching and heart healing. I wouldn't have wanted it to be with anyone but you! Write a book they said, it would be fun they said! Seriously though we did it. We got through it, we made it. Thank you from every place in my heart and being. Love you to the moon and back.

To all the staff at the Staybridge Suites in North Brunswick, NJ and Home2 Suites by Hilton in Edison, NJ. Maura and I locked ourselves in these two awesome places on two separate weekends, we wrote, cried, laughed, and got it done. The staff at both places were accommodating, professional and kind. A shout out to the Barrett Paradise Friendly Library in Cresco, Pa. We spent quite a few days writing and editing in this awesome library.

Justin Holtkamp, best friend, and husband. From the first moment we met when the universe shifted my life was never the same again. Through all the ups and downs, long distance for years to finally living together, you have been my steady. I learn from you every day whether you know it or not, that never matters. I love you always, from the depths of my heart. Thank you for your unending love, support and friendship.

I know I may have forgotten some people by name, it's not intentional. Each person that has walked through my life has a memory inside of me. I apologize in advance for missing you, but you all know who you are. If I know you and you know me, thank you for being in my life for however long or short.

About the Authors

About Maura

Maura is an Author, Angel Channeler, Teacher, Past Life Regression Practitioner, Healer, Certified Hypnosis & NLP Coach. With over 22 years experience, she is dedicated to supporting a growing Spiritual Community both online and in person. Maura lives near the beaches of New Jersey. Her Mission is to assist people on their individual healing journey; believing we can help raise the vibration of the planet, and always strive for love, kindness, and inclusion. Together we can create a life where everyone is welcome.

About Ann

Ann Merli is dedicated to supporting people with love, compassion, and kindness. Her mission is to connect with others, create community, and make the healing journey accessible to everyone. Ann has been writing since her teens, always dreaming of publishing a book. She is grateful for the opportunity to share her healing journey, hoping it inspires others to find balance and harmony.

Ann is a Reiki Master Practitioner/Teacher, Licensed Massage Therapist, and RYT500 Yoga Instructor. She has an active in-person and online energy healing practice, and teaches yoga in studio and online. She lives with her husband, Justin, and their two rescue cats, Pippy and Mitzy in the Pocono Mountains of Pennsylvania.

Printed in the USA
CPSIA information can be obtained
at www.ICGtesting.com
LVHW010755101024
793140LV00008B/29